IRISH DAYS, INDIAN MEMORIES

This book is dedicated to Kalyan Chakravarthi Golla who lived out Giri's wish to travel from Dublin to Philadelphia in search of further learning.

Irish Days, Indian Memories

V. V. Giri and Indian Law Students at University College Dublin, 1913–16

Conor Mulvagh

Irish Academic Press

First published in 2016 by
Irish Academic Press
8 Chapel Lane
Sallins
Co. Kildare
Ireland

British Library Cataloguing in Publication Data
An entry can be found on request

978-1-911024-18-7 (cloth)
978-1-911024-19-4 (PDF)
978-1-911024-20-0 (epub)
978-1-911024-21-7 (kindle)

Library of Congress Cataloging in Publication Data. An entry can be found on request.

Although my student life at the University was spent, ostensibly, for the study of law and the pursuit of Jurisprudence, I was drawn irresistibly into the cross currents of the Irish struggle

– Varahagiri Venkata Giri[1]

Contents

List of Abbreviations

BL	British Library
BMH	Bureau of Military History
CSORP	Chief Secretary's Office Registered Papers
DFA	Department of Foreign Affairs
DMP	Dublin Metropolitan Police
IOR/L/P&J	India Office Records and Private Papers, India Office: Public and Judicial Department Records, 1795–1950
IRB	Irish Republican Brotherhood
NAI	National Archives of Ireland
TCD	Trinity College Dublin
UCD	University College Dublin
UCDA	University College Dublin Archives
UKNA	National Archives (United Kingdom), Kew, London
WS	Witness Statement

Acknowledgements

This book began life in the spring of 2014 when, freshly started in a lectureship at UCD, I was asked to verify whether or not V. V. Giri, the fourth president of India, had studied at the University prior to the 1916 Rising. Little did I imagine that what started out as such a small task would open into a fascinating journey of discovery into an almost forgotten episode in the deeply connected histories of India and Ireland. Firstly, I would like to thank John McCafferty, John O'Dowd, Una Watkins and Lorraine Woods for starting me on that path and for their patience and encouragement as this project grew and developed. I was lucky and deeply grateful to have received the advice and assistance of Kate O'Malley and Gajendra Singh in the course of my research. They gave generously of their time and expertise in helping me track down new literature and sources of which I knew so little at the outset. Likewise Matt Perry, Padraig Yeates, Declan Downey and Maurice J. Bric have provided very useful insights throughout this project. I am especially grateful to Professor Bric who was kind enough to present me with his own autographed photo portrait of Giri which he had received many years before. Special thanks to Eve Morrison and Eunan O'Halpin for offering their comments on the text. I am deeply grateful to Spurti Subramanyam for her assistance in researching the lives of some of Dublin's Indian students following their return to India and to Colm O'Flaherty for his diligent work in sourcing and reproducing the images presented here.

I further wish to thank all the staff at UCD Archives, Paul Kelly and the office of the President of UCD for permission to consult the minutes of UCD's Governing Body and Academic Council; and to Professor Orla Feely and UCD Research. At the King's Inns my thanks go to Juliane Galle and Síle O'Shea, all the staff of the National Library of Ireland, the National Archives, Trinity College Dublin Library and the Departments of Early Printed Books and Manuscripts, and the Jesuit Archives in Dublin who were extremely helpful as always. In London, my thanks are due to the British Library and the staff of the Asian and African Studies Reading Room as well as to James Broadhead and Karrie Keogh for welcoming me into their home during my time researching there. At Irish Academic Press, my sincere thanks go to Conor Graham and his colleagues. To my family, my first draft editors and constant encouragers – Daragh, Deirdre, Clíona and Aoife – my thanks as always. My special thanks to Thea for her love and support.

Finally, this book is dedicated to my good friend Kalyan Chakravarthi Golla. In his memoir, V. V. Giri wrote of his last days in Dublin: '[I] was expecting to finish my courses in the University and later go to Philadelphia to study for my Master of Law degree.'[2] War, revolution and politics meant that Giri's wish to travel onwards from Ireland to the United States was never fulfilled. Instead he returned home to Berhampore where he threw himself into the Indian independence struggle. Almost a century later, having been awarded his PhD in Dublin, Kalyan travelled onwards to Philadelphia, where he is now a postdoctoral researcher in Thomas Jefferson University. In your next adventure Kalyan, I send you my best wishes.

Conor Mulvagh
University College Dublin
November 2015

Foreword

I was all of nine years studying at an Irish Catholic school when I first started thinking about the name Giri. In school, as well as public functions and social get-togethers, I would be referred to as Giri's grandson.

As I grew up, I realised I had been born into a political family and Giri was a household name in most parts of India. In the 1950s and 60s, many recognised Giri as India's trade union leader, as one who took part in the Quit India Movement, and as one elected to the Constituent Assembly as a Cabinet Minister for Labour in independent India's first cabinet. To those who were born in the late 1960s and 70s, the name Dr Varahagiri Venkata Giri meant The President of India.

As I entered my teens, I engaged with Giri and asked him several questions on global, national and local issues. His responses, anecdotes and guidance remain today a precious source of my recollections of his student days in Ireland; and those of Giri as a presidential candidate, a politician, a strategist, a nationalist leader, an empathiser with the poor and the industrial workers, a socialist at heart, a pragmatist in achieving his goals, one who spoke well of his opponents, an orator and a family man.

Giri held the view that one of the requisites of a parliamentary system of governance was not just the practice of tolerance but the need to celebrate our differences, particularly in public life. During his presidential campaign and in later years, I vividly recollect his enthusiasm and capacity to connect with several national leaders and political parties. I had the opportunity to closely observe his interaction with those who differed with him on the ways and means of resolving political issues.

Taking risks and espousing a cause came naturally to Giri. His commitment to a cause would be so intense that many a time he would take great risks to achieve his goals. In 1913, when he was just 19 and a student at the University College Dublin he - directly or indirectly - supported the Irish to attain Home Rule. And, at age 75 and much against the advice of political experts and his well-wishers, Giri decided to contest the post of President of India as an independent candidate. Until today, no one has held office as the acting President of India and nor has any independent candidate won in India's presidential elections. This was a first in the history of Indian politics.

In the early 1900s, a foreign education used to be the birth right of the privileged rich. Today, Indian students have easy access and far greater opportunities to study overseas. This very welcome book by Dr Conor Mulvagh and University College Dublin provides a deep insight into the life and times of Indian students in Ireland at that time, with Giri as its focal point.

While the challenges faced by Indian students today, globally and nationally, are quite different from those faced by Giri and his peers, there is no doubt that those who read this book, particularly Irish and Indian students, will be hugely inspired by Giri's courage and conviction. He was a student who not only integrated with the Irish people but was totally immersed in their local issues - even politically sensitive issues that may have landed him in prison.

Giri always spoke of the hospitality of the local Irish families during his stay in Dublin. He often mentioned that neither he nor the other Indian students experienced any discrimination or racial prejudice. Possibly somewhere in his mind he compared his situation as a student to that of the experiences of Indian students studying in England in the early 1900s.

Today, members of the student fraternity are possibly overwhelmed with the speed of change. In their daily lives they witness evolutionary and revolutionary changes occurring the world over, not only in the political sphere but more often in the world of technology. Books like *Irish Days, Indian Memories* may give them an insight into the tough choices some students made in the 1900s as well as the risks and sacrifices they undertook.

Even now when many books on Ireland in 1916 are appearing, there are some that will stand the test of time and remain required reading. Dr Conor Mulvagh's book is one such account. The more I read through the pages, the more I get to walk down a memory lane laced with anecdotes I heard from my grandfather about Irish-Indian relationships of the past.

Amba Preetham Parigi
Group CEO - Network18
Grandson of former President of India Dr V.V. Giri
December 2015
Mumbai, India

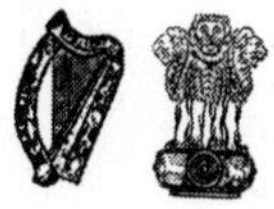

Introduction

In writing a history of the intersections between Irish and Indian nationality, this book is intended to appeal to two different audiences. To Irish readers, this short book offers an insight into a virtually unknown section of Dublin's political and student life between 1913 and 1916. Among them was V. V. Giri, fourth President of India (1969–74) who would later say of himself 'when I am not an Indian, I am an Irishman'.[1] The diversity of Dublin in this era is something which still warrants analysis and it is hoped that this study will incorporate the story of Indian students into Ireland's wartime and insurrectionary experiences. In charting the social history of Dublin as lived by Indian students in this era, I have endeavoured to present the positive and negative aspects of these interactions without dilution and, I hope, with a balance that reflects accurately the realities of the time. I am conscious that the negative aspects of encounter have a propensity to be over-represented in the archive. It is thus important to state that the best overall evidence of how well Indian students integrated into Irish life can be found in the fact that so many of their contemporaries and classmates treated them as equals and that they progressed through their studies in Dublin as peers, finding acceptance and friendship not only in the lecture theatre but in student societies, at the dinner table and in the social outlets of the city.

To Indian readers, it is hoped that what is offered here is a detailed insight into the Irish experiences of V. V. Giri, whose three-year stay in Dublin to study law between 1913 and 1916 left a lifetime legacy. Giri was one of UCD's first identifiable groups of international students. He arrived in Dublin in the late summer of 1913 along with twelve other Indian students. While the fact that Giri studied in Dublin is well known in India, the details of his time here remain impressionistic in the historiography. Furthermore, the retrospective prominence of Giri among Dublin's Indian students has served to eclipse his compatriots who joined him here to live and study. I hope that this book goes some way to uncovering some of those occluded stories and, by so doing, adds depth and context to the story of V. V. Giri's Dublin days.

Writing the history of Indian students in pre-independence Ireland has been a challenging but highly rewarding exercise. For one accustomed to standing on firmer historical ground, this study has forced me to venture further away from archival *terra firma* than usual. On the face of it, the persons at the centre of this study are almost ghosts. They have left their names in the records of the institutions in which they studied, their lodging houses have been found, and other valuable snippets of functional contemporary detail about their lives have been uncovered. However, as to their lived experiences in Dublin of a century ago, the author has been forced to rely on very scant material indeed. Thankfully this has been enhanced by the existence of a variety of memoirs and oral testimony written and recorded decades after the fact.

It is important to emphasise that this is by no means a definitive study of Indian law students in Dublin. Really, it only represents a starting point which I hope will be of benefit to scholars working on the diversity of Dublin life in this period and also to those interested in the history of international education in Ireland. Only those students who attended UCD are included in this study. By definition, these students also studied at the King's Inns but, as will be shown, a number of Indian students combined their studies at the King's Inns with periods of study at Trinity College Dublin and, it seems, British universities as well. This study finds a logical end-point in 1916. However, Indian law students built lasting associations with Dublin. It stands to future scholars to write a fuller history of these connections and to write the history of international legal education in Dublin more generally.

V. V. Giri, the figure at the centre of this study, left a vivid and lively account of his Dublin days in his autobiography, written in the 1970s. It was difficult to substantiate much of what Giri recounted in this memoir. On first reading, much of what he claimed seemed too fantastic to be true. The fact that Giri's presidential staff had written to the Irish Department of Foreign Affairs in 1972 and 1973 requesting books on Irish history to assist Giri in the composition of his memoirs raises a question mark over the originality of Giri's recollections. However, time and again, the claims made by Giri have been substantiated, often in unlikely places. A catalogue of Indian proscribed tracts proved the existence of a pamphlet of which Giri claimed to have been one of the leading organisers; the claim that Thomas MacDonagh lectured Giri has been supported by minutes in the records of UCD's Academic Council; furthermore, links between Indian students and the Irish Volunteers have also been verified. In this light, those elements which remain unsubstantiated by archival sources such as police raids and the facts around Giri's deportation become less far-fetched. Despite the amount of time which has elapsed since Ireland's revolutionary decade, new material continues to surface or be released which will perhaps shed further light on aspects of Giri's story in years to come. In uncovering links between Irish and Indian nationalists, the release of the Bureau of Military History witness statements by Ireland's Military Archives in recent years has provided essential substantiating evidence. This army-led oral history project about Ireland's revolutionary period was conducted in the late 1940s and early 1950s but only made public in 2003. These types of source provide new information about the nature and depth of Irish–Indian connections.

Although Giri takes centre stage in this study, to position him thusly is to read history backwards. While in Dublin, his greatest achievements were yet in front of him and he represented just one among fifty Indian students who studied between the King's Inns and UCD in the years 1913–17. Prior to putting flesh on the bones of Giri's compatriots, one methodological error to which I must confess is that I initially regarded Giri's Indian classmates as a monolith. This was a false conception reinforced by archival sources which so often referred to these scholars as 'Indian students', 'a number of students from Madras', and in other such terms. Even in his memoir, Giri is guilty of conflating the 'I' and the 'we' when referring to the actions of himself and his comrades. What became clear once I began to extract personalities from the list of names before me was the point which should have been obvious from the beginning, that in these fifty students held at least as many different outlooks. I began to account for the seeming incongruities between the stances of one and another anonymous Indian author appearing in the various contemporary Dublin newspapers and magazines. Through this, I realised the diversity of opinion existing among Dublin's small Indian student community. Ranging from reformers to radicals, these students held a wide cross-section of opinions. What did unite them was the need to act collectively to overcome some of the challenges they faced in Dublin. Beginning with administrative obstacles and the conservativism of members of the educational establishment and concluding with the fears over their being singled out among Dublin's citizenry, the experience of Indian students in Dublin was not without its challenges.

This book is thus as much a study of students and migration as it is one about Irish–Indian relations. The issues and problems it considers echo the questions about student activism and the difficulties of assimilation and the isolation faced by minority ethnic student communities across European cities in the same period. The longer history of Indian students in Britain and Ireland opens revealing insights, especially into the attitudes of host communities where everything from housing, moral crises, inter-racial relations, political subversion, intelligence gathering and political violence come under the spotlight. These same tropes emerge in Goetz Nordbruch's study of Arab students in Weimar Germany and Thomas Weber's *Our Friend 'The Enemy': Elite Education in Britain and Germany before World War I.*[2] Similar issues can be found in older studies on the experience of African students in the USSR, Filipino students in 1940s Chicago, and even the reaction to American (male) students in Paris during and directly after the First World War.[3]

Antoinette Burton has done important work in challenging the conception 'that the phenomenon of colonial "natives" in the [British] metropole is a twentieth century phenomenon from which the Victorian period can be hermetically sealed off.'[4] Early twentieth-century Dublin, although by no means as culturally diverse as London and British port cities such as Liverpool and Southampton, is nonetheless another example of a city in which the ethnic diversity of the metropolis has not been fully incorporated into general narratives by historians.[5] While fictional non-natives such as Leopold Bloom have earned their place in Irish public perceptions of the past, real-world analogues such as the Jewish solicitor Michael Noyk, who moved to Ireland in 1908 and became a trusted friend and confidante of advanced nationalists including Arthur Griffith, have been less readily embraced in the grand narrative of Irish history.[6]

The students under consideration here are those who came to study at University College Dublin, an institution in its infancy in this period. Building on an educational tradition which stretched back to the 1850s, UCD was still in the process of asserting and articulating its identity as the 'national' university when its first influx of international students applied to enter in the autumn of 1913. UCD was the successor to the 'University College' of the Royal University of Ireland (1882–1908) and, before that, the Catholic University founded by Cardinal John Henry Newman in 1854.[7] University College was re-constituted in 1908 with the passage of the Universities (Ireland) Act. The Act established a new National University of Ireland, replacing the old Queen's Colleges of Cork, Galway and Maynooth as well as the Royal University of Ireland, alma mater to James Joyce and other notable alumni of the late nineteenth and early twentieth centuries. Additionally, the Universities (Ireland) Act established a second new university, Queen's University Belfast, which descended from the former Queen's College there.

Returning to Dublin, the newly constituted UCD stood on the site of its predecessor but the organisational structure of the university had been changed dramatically. New professorships and faculties were established and the 'national' character of the new university was asserted in subjects such as history and the Irish language. In an important change in the new university, the Irish language also became a requisite subject for matriculation. This condition of entry lent a distinctive nationalistic character to the new university. Enthusiasm for the Irish language tended to be strong among those of a nationalist political persuasion. Before the radicalisation and transformation of Irish politics that occurred in the latter half of the First World War, the student body of UCD was, like the majority of Irish society, largely supportive of the peaceful and constitutional Irish Home Rule movement which boasted consistent control over roughly three-quarters of Ireland's

103 seats in the House of Commons between 1885 and 1918. Among the new university's staff the Professor of National Economics, Tom Kettle, and the Professor of Constitutional Law and the Law of Public and Private Wrongs, John Gordon Swift MacNeill, were both Home Rule MPs in this period.[8]

In spite of the prevailing dominance of orthodox nationalist politics in UCD, between 1913 and 1914, the fledgling university also produced new militant movements. While ideologically loyal to the Home Rule tradition, these individuals and groups inaugurated a radical departure from constitutionalism in their tactics. In November 1913, Eoin MacNeill, Professor of Early (including Mediaeval) Irish History, became the leader of a newly founded paramilitary organisation, the Irish Volunteers. The force was pledged to the defence of Irish Home Rule. In April of 1914, MacNeill's initiative was followed up by his colleague, Agnes O'Farrelly, lecturer, and later professor, of Irish at UCD. O'Farrelly was a leading founding member of Cumann na mBan, the women's auxiliary to the Irish Volunteers. Both the men's Irish Volunteers and the women's Cumann na mBan trained their members in the use of arms. Although the university itself was keen to show its support for the war effort after Britain declared war on Germany on 4 August 1914, individual members of the college staff were heavily involved in more radical politics. In April 1916, an insurrection broke out in Dublin and an Irish Republic was proclaimed; the University found itself in the unusual situation of having to formulate a response to the fact that several of its staff had been arrested for their role in the rebellion.[9] Among the leadership of the rebellion was Thomas MacDonagh, assistant lecturer in English at UCD and commandant of the 2nd Dublin Battalion of the Irish Volunteers. As a signatory of the document proclaiming the Irish Republic and as commander of one of the rebel garrisons, MacDonagh was among fourteen executed in Dublin following the surrender of the self-proclaimed provisional government.

As to the student body in UCD, taking the figures for 1915, there were 946 students in total: 722 men and 224 women. The largest faculties were Arts-Science-Commerce, which had an enrolment of 437, and Medicine which – even with the diminution of student numbers during the First World War – had 292 students.[10] The Law faculty in 1915 numbered sixty-six students of whom only one was a woman, women being ineligible to membership of the Honourable Society of King's Inns at the time thus precluding them from practicing law as barristers.[11] Of these sixty-six, thirty-four were studying for a full degree course in Law at UCD while the other forty-nine, including twenty-four Indian students, were attending lectures at UCD for the period of a year in order to fulfil the requirements of the King's Inns which conferred and governed membership of the outer and inner Bars of Ireland.[12] This, the highest year of Indian enrolment at UCD, saw Indian law students constituting more than a third of all law students and just less than half of the 'other' law students at UCD.

These Indian students also undertook legal studies in order to qualify for the Bar at the Honourable Society of the King's Inns, Dublin. A much older institution than UCD, the Honourable Society of King's Inns had been established in 1541 and had moved to the site it presently occupies on Constitution Hill in the 1790s. Up until 1867, the King's Inns catered for barristers, solicitors, attorneys and law students. However, from 1868 onwards, it only represented the barrister profession and students wishing to be called to the Bar.[13] Up until 1885, students studying to be called to the Irish Bar were obliged to reside at one of the four English inns of court at London as a prerequisite to qualification.[14]

In a final note, while this restriction had been lifted prior to the period during which Indian students travelled to Dublin to study at the King's Inns, one other major reform was yet on the horizon. Whereas both UCD and TCD were open to female students by 1913, the King's Inns maintained a strict gender bar. The Benchers, who acted as the governing body of the King's Inns, were resistant on this front. Ultimately, external legislation changed the regime at the Inns and the Sex Disqualification (Removal) Act (1919) facilitated the entry of women students. The first woman to be called to the Irish Bar was Frances Christian Kyle, who was called in November 1921.[15] While Indian students were arriving at King's Inns in the autumn of 1913, the Irish Womens' Reform League wrote to the Benchers requesting that a deputation be received to appeal to the Society to admit women. The Benchers informed the Under-Treasurer of the Society to acknowledge the correspondence received 'and to inform the League that the law does not allow women to become students or Barristers-at-Law, and that as no good purpose would be served by receiving a deputation the Benchers must decline according to the request'.[16] At a time when the first large-scale influx of Indian students was occurring at the King's Inns, it is interesting to see the resistance of the Society to a further diversification of the student body.

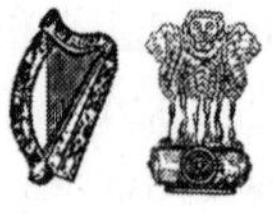

Chapter 1

Irish and Imperial Contexts

Despite the vast geographic distance between Ireland and India, the two countries share much in common experience. Imperialism, the demand for Home Rule, independence, partition and the incremental achievement of sovereignty are all common tropes in the stories of these former colonies of the British Empire. Decolonisation and the formation of so-called nation-states was, arguably, the most dominant historical force in the politics of the twentieth century. The movements that agitated for independence from kingdoms, empires and commonwealths in the period were led by men and women with a detailed knowledge of the regimes against which they were fighting. University education played a major role, not only in creating educated and socially conscious young agitators who contributed to the new politics of their day, but also in establishing networks where those interested in different but invariably related causes could meet and associate.

Home Rule had been the dominant force in Irish political life between 1885 and 1918. Loosely analogous with the Indian term Swaraj, 'self-rule', the linkages between the two movements are not merely linguistic. The Irish Home Rule MP Frank Hugh O'Donnell had founded the Indian

Constitutional Association in 1882 and had established contact with the mainly student-led London Indian Society which had been founded a decade previously.[1] O'Donnell's interest in India was by no means half-hearted. Although it ultimately came to nothing, the most ambitious plan for an Irish–Indian alliance proposed that four Indians be selected to represent Irish constituencies in parliament at Westminster in a mutual pact that would see Irish MPs support all Indian legislation while the Indians would be obliged to provide representation to their constituents and to lend support to the Irish campaign for Home Rule.[2]

In 1913, a tumultuous year in Irish political life, a group of Indian students arrived in Dublin city. They enrolled at the Honourable Society of the King's Inns to study for the Bar. Additionally, they enrolled at University College Dublin, a constituent college of the National University of Ireland. This group of Indian students appears to have been the first bulk influx of international students to the new university arriving from a single country to study a single subject. In the history of international education in Ireland, this constituted an important chapter.

The subject chosen by these Indian students was not arbitrary. For many years prior to their arrival, law had been the subject of choice for Indians travelling abroad for study and those who were interested in the Indian national cause. Although the historian Alex Tickell points to the politicising impact of study of the law due to its ability to expose the student to the disparity between British and Indian legal systems, Shompa Lahiri offers a more pragmatic reason for the popularity of legal study among Indian students.[3] Lahiri states that 'the popularity of law among Indian students [in Britain] was due to the privileged position English-trained barristers exercised over Indian-qualified pleaders'.[4] Furthermore, Lahiri claims that 'Bar examinations were even said to be easier than legal examinations in India.'[5]

In London, the National Indian Association estimated that there were more than 160 Indian students in British Universities by 1885, a number that had risen to 700 by 1910.[6] Elsewhere, Lahiri has written that, owing to the fact that no formal census of Indian students in Britain was ever taken, figures can vary widely and accuracy in numbers remains elusive. Lahiri does, however, produce a table, working from the best available sources – the Journal of the National Indian Association and the Indian Student Department report which will be considered in greater depth later. From a base figure of 40–50 students in 1873 – more than a decade before Burton's count on students begins – Lahiri sees the number of students growing slowly from 100 in 1880 to no more than 400 by the turn of the century. However, 700–800 in 1907 more than doubled to 1,700–1,800 by 1913 which represents a high water mark. In 1922 there were an estimated 1,500 students with numbers not returning to 1,800 until 1927.[7]

Underlining the importance of legal study to the Indian student community, Antoinette Burton observes that Indian students in London gravitated towards Bloomsbury. This neighbourhood was close to the British Library, the Inns of Court and Temple Bar.[8] A Parliamentary Report from the India Students' Department for 1913–14 estimates a total of 1,600 to 1,700 Indian students studying in British institutions in this period. In 1914, 609 of these were registered at the Inns of Court in London, meaning that law students accounted for almost two-fifths of all Indian students in Britain at that time.[9]

In his autobiography, V. V. Giri recalls how 'Indian students preferred to study in Ireland in preference to England because there was neither a colour bar nor racial prejudice of any kind among the Irish, probably due to the adverse circumstances of their history.'[10] Lending support to Giri's impression that Ireland was a more welcoming destination for Indian students, the Indian Students' Department's report notes that, while the figure for law students entering London's Inns of Court in

1913 was 609, 'the number of new students who have joined the Inns in the last twelve months shows a sensible decline. At Dublin the number of Law students at the King's Inns had risen on the same date to 17.'[11] Thus there is some empirical basis for Giri's claim that attitudes to studying in England were changing at this point and that, for a small number of student pioneers, Ireland was considered an attractive alternative.

On the existence of a racial and colour bar in England, the Indian Students' Department also has information to offer. In a tone that fluctuates between the defensive and the patronising, the Indian Students' Department reported that

> Some Indian students not unnaturally expect that facilities for joining English institutions like the Universities ... will be thrown open to them as a matter of right and are disappointed to find that so many formalities have to be complied with first ... these institutions are independent bodies, with distinctive rules and traditions of their own, free to lay down any conditions they like for the admission of any class of students, and, it may be slow to act when asked to throw open to students from the other side of the world privileges that were once reserved for limited classes of English people.[12]

Admitting the inequality of the system, the Committee urged Indian students 'to comply with the regulations imposed, while doing all that can be done to break down prejudice and to alter any conditions that are illiberal or unfair'.[13]

Alex Tickell also examines the moral dimensions of British perceptions of Indian students in the early twentieth century. He details how popular literature emphasised the mixture of fear and fascination about Indian life in the metropolis. Story lines frequently mixed themes of seditious plotting with moral panic over liaisons between white women and Indian men. Such topics were not merely the fodder for potboiler novellas, the same concerns about morality, assimilation and the excess of liberty which young Indian (male) students supposedly had in Britain led to the establishment of a committee of investigation into Indian students in Britain.[14]

The Lee Warner Committee reported to government in 1907 (although the findings were not made public until 1922) and suggested that Indian students be housed with 'respectable' English families so as to afford a degree of paternalistic guidance, oversight and control that would mitigate against the dangers of either political or sexual expression as the drafters behind this report saw it.[15] The report recommended the establishment of an advisory board and a bureau of information for subcontinental students which resulted in the establishment of a new Indian Students' Department within the India Office in London.[16]

The Indian Students' Department was, however, found to be more of an agency of surveillance and control than of assistance to Indian students. By 1913, some of Britain's Indian students were complaining that the India Office and its constituent Indian Students' Department were actually at the centre of this 'illiberal' and 'unfair' regime of entry requirements and background checks to which Indian students in Britain were being subjected. Lacking other means of accrediting incoming Indian students, institutions of learning, hospitals and the Inns of Court began to require clearance from the India Office or the Indian Students' Department on a student's suitability. Local advisers had been appointed to work with the Indian students at Oxford, Cambridge, Manchester, Glasgow and Edinburgh Universities in 1913. However, Shompa Lahiri explains that the students made formal representations against these advisers and they were replaced by the universities' own advisers as a result.[17]

Interestingly, within only a few months of Indian students having arrived in Dublin, the same sentiments were being expressed by figures within the Irish establishment in the pages of Dublin's southern unionist newspaper, the *Irish Times*. An article published on 17 April 1914 questioned whether more stringent regulations as to the admittance of Indian students to Dublin's King's Inns would be a 'wise and necessary measure'.[18] Fearing that the recent tightening up of regulations in the Inns of Court in London would mean that 'if there be any undesirable Indian students in these countries, they would tend, under the existing regulations, to find their way to Dublin'.[19] It is revealing that the author of this piece was not concerned about academic standards at the King's Inns slipping but rather about Indian 'undesirables' making Dublin a destination of choice.

It was not only academic interest and career advancement that saw a large proportion of Indian students in Britain and Ireland choose law. One of the objects of Indian nationalists who encouraged and sometimes funded young Indians to travel to the British Isles for study was to expose these young men first hand to the difference between the Indian and British legal systems.[20] The Indian legal code included many laws which did not have a counterpart in Britain. Penalties and sentences under Indian law were markedly harsher than those which existed under the justice system at the centre of the empire in Britain.

Ireland and Scotland had, like India, region-specific legal codes. Part of the justification for the disparity of legal codes for regions within the United Kingdom was attributed to the religious distinctiveness both of Ireland, with its Catholic majority, and of Scotland with its predominance of Presbyterians, dissenters and non-conformists. Thus culturally sensitive areas like education and the licensing of liquor were given different treatment in England and Wales than they were under Irish and Scottish law. However, regional disparity in the law was also used to impose restrictions in Ireland which would not have been tolerated in Britain. Among these were restrictions on the ownership and importation of firearms – something paralleled by legislation in India – and the exception of Ireland from the territorial system which saw an overhaul of army reservists and militias in Britain in 1907. In both Ireland and India, coercion bills had been introduced following waves of political agitation, most notably following the 1857 India mutiny and the Irish Fenian uprising of 1867. Agrarian as well as political agitation were common to both Ireland and India. In Ireland, a raft of legislation was passed between 1870 and 1909 which offered both carrot and stick to the Irish tenant farmer transforming Irish land holdings from a tenanted model to the principle of owner-occupier. Despite being slow and relatively lacking in violence, the gradual resolution of the Irish land question precipitated the most far-reaching social revolution seen in modern Irish history.

Chapter 2

Changing Attitudes to Indians in Britain, 1907–13

University education in Ireland had been radically overhauled in 1908 with the passing of the Irish Universities Act. A constituent college of the new National University of Ireland, the reconstituted UCD opened its doors to its first students in 1909. However, word of Ireland's great university reforms is unlikely to have been the reason why Indian students were beginning to look beyond the more established English universities for their education. A very different event in 1909 appears to have signalled the alteration of conditions faced by Indian students in the British Isles.

On 1 July 1909, while attending an evening's entertainment for the National Indian Association at the Imperial Institute, South Kensington, London, Sir William Hutt Curzon Wyllie, a senior official in the British Government of India, was shot and instantly killed by a Punjabi student studying engineering at London University, Madan Lal Dhingra. In the course of the attack, Dhingra also shot Dr Cawas Lalcaca, a Parsi physician, who intervened in a failed attempt to save Wyllie. The assassination caused panic in British administrative and security circles. Political assassination was not altogether uncommon in India at the time but the fact that Wyllie had been gunned down in London rather than Lahore was what shocked the British authorities. Attitudes towards Indians in Britain, especially students, soured dramatically after this point. Even before the assassination of Wyllie, Indian students had begun to be viewed with increasing suspicion by Britons.

Alex Tickell notes that a fellow student who turned police informer at Dhingra's trial claimed that the primary target at the Imperial Institute assassination may not have been Wyllie but rather William Lee-Warner. Lee-Warner was a seasoned colonial administrator, the former political and secret secretary at the India Office in London and, since 1902, member of the Secretary of State for India's Council.[1] Crucially, in 1907, Lee-Warner had chaired a committee established to inquire into the position of Indian students in Britain. The Lee-Warner Committee had interviewed Indian students in a variety of British universities in the course of its report.

There is an interesting Irish dimension to the case of Madan Lal Dhingra. Following Wyllie's murder, Irish support for the assassin came from the perhaps unlikely source of a radical bi-lingual nationalist–feminist newspaper, *Bean na hÉireann* (Woman of Ireland). In its July 1909 issue, the paper carried an article among its editorial notes entitled 'The Indian Assassination'.[2] The article aligned the plights of India and Ireland.[3] The following month the magazine lent further support to Madan Lal Dhingra:

> Madar Lal Dinghra [sic], who shot Sir Curzon Wylie [sic] in London, is to be duly hanged on the 10th of August.
>
> The assassination of the officials who exploit India and the Indian people for the enrichment of England is an eventuality that the English had not reckoned on. For the Indian to retaliate when he was kicked like a dog is

1. Signed photo portrait of Venkata Varahagiri Giri, fourth president of India, 1969-74 (courtesy of Maurice J. Bric).

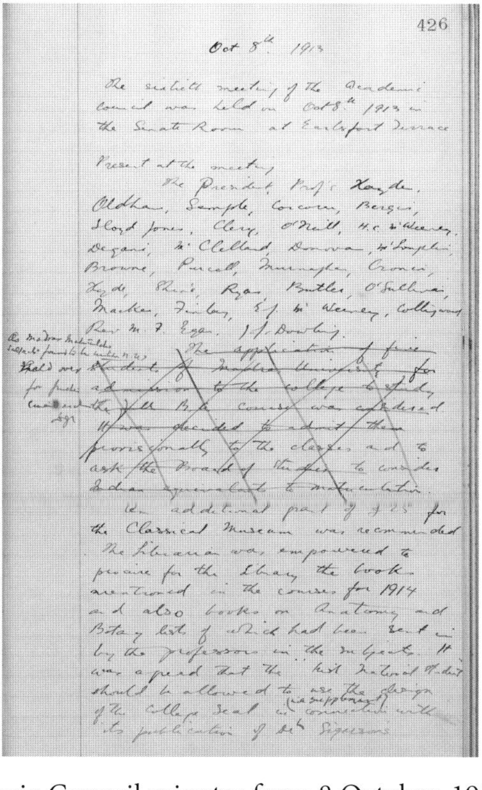

2. UCD Academic Council minutes from 8 October, 1913. The section referring to Indian students has been crossed out (IE UCDA, Gv1/1, digital image (c) UCD Digital Library, reproduced by kind permission of UCD Archives).

3. Earlsfort Terrace, the main site of UCD from 1883 until 1970 when the University began moving students to the Belfield campus in south Dublin. The last students to leave Earlsfort Terrace for Belfield did so in 2007. The University had been founded in 1854 at numbers 85 and 86 St Stephen's Green nearby. The photograph here shows Earlsfort Terrace on 3 January 1922. UCD hosted Dáil Éireann's debates on the Anglo-Irish treaty in December 1921 and January 1922 ('photo by Bobinchak', Desmond FitzGerald Photographs, P80/PH/179, digital image (c) UCD Digital Library dx.doi.org/10.7925/drs1.ucdlib_30864, reproduced by kind permission of UCD Archives).

4. A view of the Honourable Society of King's Inns building from Constitution Hill (public domain, William Murphy, Flickr creative commons).

·Bean·na·h-Eireann·

(THE WOMAN OF IRELAND)

Vol. I, No. 6.] Aibreán (APRIL), 1909. [Price One Penny.

5. The masthead of *Bean na hÉireann*, the nationalist-feminist newspaper which expressed support for Madan Lal Dhingra in 1909 (reproduced courtesy of the National Library of Ireland).

6. Helena Molony, nationalist, feminist, and trade union activist. As editor of *Bean na hÉireann*, she was prominent in the campaign supporting Madan Lal Dhingra (from R. M. Fox, *Rebel Irishwomen*).

7. 1 Grove Park, Rathmines, the house in which Giri lodged along with Shri Unnava Lakshminarayana when he first arrived in Dublin (photograph by author).

8. Lowell House, Herbert Avenue, Merrion, the house in which Giri lived from 1914 onwards according to the best available data (photograph by author).

THE ★ IRISH ★ VOLUNTEER ★

ÓGLÁC NA H-ÉIREANN ★★★

Vol. 1. No. 1. Saturday, February, 7th, 1914. Price, One Penny

Should the Recruit be Sworn?

In this question of taking in recruits there is some difference of opinion as to the best method of procedure to be adopted. It has been customary to ask each unit when joining to make a declaration, but in some districts this is not regarded as quite satisfactory. It is said that each member should be made to kiss a rifle or sword, in the presence of the corps, when making his declaration, and that that would tend to impress him more with the sacredness of his obligations towards the movement. It would, no doubt, add solemnity and have a fine spectacular effect, but at the same time very few will join the movement except with a clear conception of what is expected of them, and their declaration is sufficient bond. Of course there are precedents, legendary and actual for the other course; but, after all, it is questionable if the man who is impressed by the mere form of the declaration will be of the type that would be most scrupulous in its observance.

Uniforms.

[illegible] question of uniforms has so far been decided upon, but a sub-committee has been appointed by the Provisional Committee to deal with the matter. And simple as it seems, the question is a little difficult to solve satisfactorily. In some quarters it has been suggested that the various regiments should go back to the '82 movement for the colours at least, if not the actual cut, of the military dress, and while this idea has not met with much favour, neither has the suggestion of a simple coloured blouse with ordinary trousers and leggings. Then there is the question as to whether all Volunteers should wear a similarly coloured uniform, or will the cut alone be decided upon and the colour left to the taste of the regiments in different districts? Not very important questions these, but at the same time they are giving rise to speculation. However, this, too is a question that will be decided at an early date.

Arms.

The recent proclamation prohibiting the importation of arms into Ireland has for the immediate present been a disadvantage, though ultimately it may prove to have been a blessing in disguise. Whether it was aimed at the National Volunteers or not, its operation has handicapped the movement slightly in its initial stage. Every man who has a spark of the Volunteer spirit loves a rifle, and apart from their use as a weapon in war, the possession of a rifle rouses the enthusiasm of most recruits. At the same time anything like the wholesale purchase of rifles would have been folly, and the proclamation, perhaps, prevented that. There is little doubt that before rifles are again used in war that a vastly improved pattern will have appeared on the market, and the difficulty in getting them will be no greater than was the difficulty of getting the Mauser or Lee Enfield up to a couple of months ago. At the same time there must be quite enough rifles for drill purposes, and small, batches of Volunteers could be drilled in the various halls with borrowed rifles. But for the present everything should be subordinated to building up the movement itself, getting the men into it, seeing that they are properly disciplined and drilled, and then when they are ready and when the need arises, procuring rifles will not present so much difficulty.

"The Irish Volunteer."

We owe an apology to our readers for our tardy appearance, but the difficulties always associated with the appearance of a first number must be our excuse. We also owe an apology to contributors and correspondents who have been good enough to send us articles and reports, very many of which we have been obliged to hold over or condense unduly. This is particularly true of correspondents who sent us reports of meetings of Fianna branches and [illegible] [illegible] hope to do very much better in the future in the way of finding space for all happenings of interest to the movement. The present number is devoted mainly to Volunteer propaganda, and our readers will find different aspects of the movement ably dealt with by the different writers over whose signatures they appear. At the same time it should be clearly understood that however well a signed article may sum up any or all phases of the movement that it does not officially speak for the National Volunteer. On Page 9 of each issue will be found all official communications that the Provisional Committee wish to make to the Volunteer Corps.

A Request to Correspondents.

We would ask the hon. secs in the various districts to send us reports of the doings of their corps at the earliest moment possible. The amount of space which we will be able to devote to any report will depend largely upon the time we receive it. We go to press on Tuesday, and as many reports as possible should be sent so as to reach us as far as possible in advance of that.

Future Issues

In our next and subsequent issues we will deal with the Volunteer movement from a more practical point of view. To this end we will aim at providing every recruit with simple lessons in the various branches of training. Drill, rifles and rifle practice, semaphore signalling, ambulance work will be dealt with by experts, who will treat their various subjects simply and in plain language. "The Irish Volunteer" will be a record of the progress of the movement and an invaluable handbook for every recruit.

FROM THE OUTPOST.

The Movement Spreads.

The Volunteer movement is marching. Ranks have been formed, and with steady step and to the music of Ireland's soul the first bivouac has been made on the road to achieve its destiny. The military maps show our troops spreading through the length and breadth of the land. A regiment here, a flanking party there. In the Capital the head of a column whose rear guard invests Achill Island. Advance guards wait in the towns from Wexford to Donegal, and scouts have mapped the way to every village and reported the possibilities of success in every hamlet. In a week or a month maybe city, town and hamlet will alike be filled with our troops. Only sedition in the ranks can prevent ultimate success. And that is unthinkable. The old spirit of Nationality that has never died in Ireland has kindled again at the prospect of soldiers' work, and recruits everywhere are waiting impatiently to get the order to join the ranks. The Headquarter's Staff have been very busy so far, and it was difficult to perfect organising details, but in a couple of weeks all that will be different.

IRELAND, 1914.

(To the air of "Silent O'Moyle.")

By Padraic Colum.

The four seas of Eirinn are loud in their challenge,
This moment is lightening lake, river and flood;
The sods that we tread on are thrilling to bear us,
The winds blow—the winds blow to waken our blood.

O Banba, proud Banba, from Mumhan and Uladh,
From Laighan and Connacht and new lands beyond
Thy children are gathered—they stand for thine honour,
The sun is their banner, thy name is their bond!

The sea that is northward it clamours of conquest—
The ships of King Dathi with victories decked;
The sea that is eastward remembers King Brian,
The hopes of the Vikings are vanquished and wrecked.

O Eire, brave Eire, from Mumhan and Uladh,
From Laighan and Connacht and new lands beyond,
Thy children are gathered—they stand for thine honour,
The sun is our banner, thy name is their bond!

The sea that is southward is low in its challenge,—
We'll fail not, we'll fail not for honour of Tone!
The sea that is westward, its surge strikes Killala—
Now, now, we are ready, now our freedom we'll own!

Fola, loved Fola, from Mumhan and Uladh,
From Laighan and Connacht and new lands beyond,
Thy children are gathered—they stand for thine honour,
The sun is their banner, thy name is their bond!

The four seas of Eirinn are loud in their challenge,
This moment is lightening lake, river and flood;
The sods that we tread on are thrilling to bear us,
The winds blow—the winds blow to waken our blood!

Innisfail, Innisfail from green rath and cairn,
From lough-side and mountain thy memories come, fond,
Thy heroes are mingled with us in this hosting,
The sun is their banner, thy name is our bond!

—PADRAIC COLUM.

9. The masthead of the inaugural issue of the *Irish Volunteer,* the official newspaper of the movement of the same name, 7 February 1914. On 7 March 1914, the paper published an anonymous article entitled 'Indian Nationality' written by an Indian subsequently identified as P. S. T. Sayee, a law student (courtesy of UCD National Folklore Collection).

THE

NATIONAL STUDENT.

A MAGAZINE OF UNIVERSITY LIFE.

Conducted by the Students of University College, Dublin.

No. 16.] Vol. IV., No. 6. JUNE, 1914. THREEPENCE.

CONTENTS:

THE AWAKENING.

THERE are times when chance brings to the conduct or words of a man a significance far beyond the measure of the man or the greatness of the moment. When Mr. Balfour was speaking the final words of his speech in Parliament, on the 29th April, last, such a moment had arrived.

As a man recording in the twilight hour of his life the collapse of the hopes that had animated his political career, and assenting to the failure of his ideals, Mr. Balfour, just then, was a figure that touched the pathetic. When he asserts that, towards the making of stable relations between Ireland and England, the removal of secondary grievances, the smoothing away of inequalities, or the encouragement of industry had been to him as the light of the Grail on the marsh; that the visions of a day when these, the toil of his years, should blot out the ancient memories had proved to be vain; that the cause to which he gave his powers of mind and for which he had striven had been fated to break down; and that at the end of it all nothing to him remained but resignation to the failure of a life's work—there comes to mind the image of a man with claims to the pity of all men who themselves know the bitterness of disappointment and personal defeat.

10. The *National Student*, the UCD student magazine. This is the June 1914 issue which included an article, 'The Indian Students', anonymously written by 'An Indian' (courtesy of UCD Library).

11. Portrait of Denis J. Coffey, first President of UCD, 1909-1940 (by kind permission of the President's Office, UCD).

12. Robert Donovan, Professor of English at UCD (*Irish Independent*, 13 April 1934, reproduced courtesy of the National Library of Ireland)

13. Thomas MacDonagh, assistant lecturer in English at UCD, commandant of the 2nd (Dublin) Battalion of the Irish Volunteers and proclamation signatory. Executed, 3 May 1916 (Harris & Ewing, Public Domain).

14. Thomas A. Finlay, SJ, Professor of Political Economy at UCD (artist unknown, University College Dublin, reproduced courtesy of the Irish Jesuit Archives).

IRISH REBELLION, MAY 1916.
JAMES CONNOLLY.
(Commandant-General Dublin Division).
Executed May 9th, 1916.
One of the signatories of the 'Irish Republic Proclamation

15. James Connolly, Irish trade unionist, leader of the Irish Citizen Army and proclamation signatory. Executed 12 May 1916 (IE UCDA P34/F/3. By kind permission of UCD Archives).

> unthinkable. Now that Dinghra [sic] has retaliated on behalf of his country all England shrieks 'murderer', and he will be hanged by the neck. The epithet has been ever ready to her lips when any man has dared to pay her back in kind for the ruin she has brought on his people. The same hypocritical cry swept England when Burke and Cavendish were killed in the Phoenix Park as when Wylie [sic] was killed in London.[4]

By linking the 1882 Phoenix Park murders to Wyllie's assassination, the author was making a very clear point about the justification of retaliatory acts of violence among colonially oppressed peoples. Continuing along these lines, the anonymous author then added the plight of the Boers to a litany of imperial abuses:

> The England that has brought famine and death to untold thousands in India, that slew in her African Concentration Camp twenty thousand Boer women and children, that organised a famine in Ireland whereby two millions of our people died by the roadside of hunger and disease – this pious, Christian hypocrite, England, without pity – without shame, with nothing but her blind and boundless greed and lust for power – with her canting pretence to religion, is ever ready to brand with the foul name of murderer men who have the courage to stand against her and sacrifice their lives for the people. She has sown Dragon's Teeth and they have sprung up armed men. If political assassination be crime, the guilt belongs to those who provoke it rather than to the man who strikes back in an effort to stay the ruin of a nation. If Curzon Wylie [sic] was murdered [,] England and not Dinghra [sic] was the murderer. It is at her door the responsibility must be left. She is reaping where she has sown, and the harvest is of her own creation.[5]

Returning from Dhingra to the common experience of oppression, the author questioned not only the causes of famines but the legitimacy of government more generally before giving a final justification for Dhingra's actions:

> India, like Ireland, is systematically plundered and oppressed. When its population is inconveniently large it always happens to be swept by State-aided famine, and thousands die of hunger. Indian leaders are deported, charges are invented by perjured police, national papers are suppressed and their editors imprisoned. The strong ones of the nation are captured or killed and the weak are either purchased or intimidated. The country is given over to a horde of English officials who drain the life blood of the nation. If an Indian protests it is 'sedition', if he retaliates it is 'murder'. The same system worked in Ireland. We are familiar with its every detail. Yet we who suffer under the same blighting influence refer in our newspapers to an Indian Patriot as 'this unhappy and mis-guided man' and his action as 'fearful crime'. Surely Ireland is not going to be the contemptible echo of the arch hypocrite among nations. Rather than condemnation of Dinghra [sic] or any patriot Indian, Ireland should stretch hands of sympathy to help the Indian groaning under the same tyranny as ourselves, and we should pray and work that we like India may have men and women who are 'proud to have the honour of laying down their lives for the cause of their country'.[6]

Signed 'F.', the case that advanced political opinion in Ireland looked sympathetically upon Dhingra's actions was thus dramatically stated.

The following month, *Bean na hÉireann* began with a long article justifying physical force as a political tactic juxtaposed incongruously with its monthly 'The woman with a garden' column before offering further commentary on Irish reactions to Dhingra's execution. In the 'Editorial Notes' section of the August edition, the following appeared:

> Our complaint last month about the attitude of the Irish Press and the Irish people towards Madar Lal Dinghra [sic], the Indian patriot, was premature. The Press indeed has preserved the same neutrality, and discharged its duty to its own satisfaction by advising the Government how to prevent such incidents in future. The Irish people, however, have shown that they have a bigger conception of the nobility of this young man's sacrifice and the spirit that prompted the deed is worthy of honour in Ireland. On the day following his execution large placards bearing the following words appeared: –
>
> IRELAND HONOURS
> MADAR LAL DINGHRA [SIC]
> Who was proud to lay down his life for his country.
>
> In Dublin at least six beautiful floral wreaths appeared on our own patriots' monuments, and holy spots like St. Catherine's Church where Robert Emmet gave up his young life. We congratulate our country-men and women – for certainly those wreaths were the work of feminine fingers – who thought it fitting to honour Dinghra [sic] by decorating the monuments of our own mighty dead, who were 'proud to lay down their lives for their country'.[7]

Helena Molony, the editor of *Bean na hÉireann*, recalled her involvement in the Dhingra solidarity campaign to the Bureau of Military History with remarkable clarity forty years after the fact. In recounting her involvement in Inghínídhe na hÉireann (the Daughters of Ireland) and *Bean na hÉireann*, Molony explained:

> ... about this time a young Indian revolutionary, Madar [sic] Lal Dhingra, was captured and hanged for complicity in the assassination of a prominent Indian police official. From the dock, when sentenced, he declared, 'I am proud to lay down my life for my country'.
>
> We got printed immediate1y, and fly-posted through the City, posters stating 'Ireland honours Madar Lal Dhingra, who was proud to lay down his life for his country'. There was nothing insular about Inghínídhe's political outlook. We reproduced this poster in 'Bean na hEireann', and it resulted in the loss of some advertisements and subscriptions.[8]

It is interesting that Molony recalled Dhingra's trail as having included a patriotic speech from the dock as this is a trope which carries much significance in the Irish revolutionary tradition going back to Robert Emmet. Emmet had delivered a celebrated oration from the dock prior to his execution in 1803. The other interesting point about Molony's recollection of the episode is that the stance taken by Bean na hÉireann on Dhingra resulted in a loss of revenue for the paper. Evidently advocacy of political assassination was not generally in vogue in the Ireland of the time.

A separate witness statement in the Bureau of Military History by P. S. O'Hegarty, a prominent republican and, in these years, an important member of the London Gaelic League, adds a further layer to the story of Irish nationalist women's interest in the cause of Madan Lal Dhingra. O'Hegarty suggests a potential point of contact between Irish and Indian nationalists resident in London at the home of a Mrs Dryhurst. Mrs Dryhurst was the wife of an official in the British Museum and, to quote O'Hegarty, she was 'sympathetic with "any good cause at all", in Thomas Davis' sense, and especially the small oppressed nations'. Mrs Dryhurst was, likewise, a member of the Gaelic League in London and O'Hegarty recollects that 'it is seldom that there was not a political refugee from the Baltic, from India, or from Georgia, in the house. And she was in everything Irish helping in everything, running little concerts, lending her drawing-room for rehearsals of plays, and so on.'[9] In searching for the elusive meeting places of Indian and Irish nationalists, Dryhurst's home in London is an obvious contender. However, Dryhurst's involvement with the Dhingra case goes much deeper than her role as a radical salon-host. O'Hegarty states:

> I do not recollect the year but it might have been round about 1908. An Indian, Nader Lal Dhingra [sic], had shot a British official in England and had been convicted and was awaiting execution in, I think Brixton Jail, or at any rate somewhere in South London. Mrs. Dryhurst got the notion of rescuing him and asked us to bear a hand. She had it all planned. She had discovered that, every day about the same time, Dhingra was taken out somewhere near the prison along a road which was fairly unfrequented, and accompanied by only two warders who appeared to be unarmed, in a slow-moving vehicle. The idea was to hold the party up with two empty revolvers which she had procured somewhere and get Dhingra well away before releasing the warden, and we were asked to find six boys and two girls for the purpose, the girls to walk with the boys so that it would not look like a party. All arrangements were made, and the thing looked feasible enough on Mrs. Dryhurst's premise, but a couple of days before the execution – the rescue was planned for the day before – Dhingra was moved to another prison, and there was nothing to be done. We had such faith in Mrs. Dryhurst that we went into this at her request without any attempt to check up on the particulars which she disclosed and on which the plan was based.[10]

On top of her Indian sympathies, Mrs Dryhurst was involved in the early days of *Bean na hÉireann*, thus providing another tangible link between the paper and the case of Dhingra. The Dhingra case sent a clear signal, especially to Indians in London, that Irish advanced nationalists, especially or even exclusively suffragists at this point, found common cause in the plights of Ireland and India. In the case of Dryhurst, these activists were even willing to work outside the law in offering practical assistance to Indian political activists. In a history in which so few concrete links can be established, the case of Irish nationalist-feminists and their solidarity with Madan Lal Dhingra provides the most likely avenue of approach between Irish and Indian activists in London at a time when Britain was becoming a cold house for incoming Indian students. It would seem this type of connection may well have played a role in the decision of Indian law students to travel to Ireland to undertake their studies four years later in 1913.

The other strong Indo-Irish connection at around this time centred on Rabindranath Tagore, the Bengali poet who came to the attention of W. B. Yeats in 1912. Yeats was captivated by Tagore's writings which he read in translation 'in railway trains, or on the top of omnibuses and in restaurants, and I have often had to close [the manuscript] lest some stranger would see how much it moved me'.[11] Yeats championed Tagore, writing a laudatory introduction to his collection of poems published by the India Society in London in the autumn of 1912. In his exploration of the Yeats–Tagore relationship, Malcolm Sen records that Tagore's collection was reprinted a dozen times within a year. Yeats' introduction, notes Sen, is 'exemplary of western conceptions of the Orient'.[12] Arguably what Yeats found in Tagore's writings was an apparent spiritual simplicity reminiscent of what he had 'discovered' in the west of Ireland years previously. In any case, Yeats' patronage was instrumental to Tagore being awarded the Nobel Prize for Literature in 1913, a full decade before Yeats himself was bestowed with the same honour. Given the international prominence which the award gave to Tagore in 1913, this is just one other possible reason why Ireland may have sparked the interest of prospective law students either at home or lingering in London and contemplating their choices of institution. In a concluding note on Tagore and Ireland, in 2011, a bust of the poet was presented to the Irish government by the government of India and was put on display in Dublin's St Stephen's Green.[13] Perhaps appropriately, the site chosen for the bust is directly across the road from the original premises of UCD where Giri and his Indian classmates would have studied almost a century beforehand.

Chapter 3

Indian Law Students Arrive in Ireland

There were 3,606 persons of Indian birth living in Ireland at the time of the 1911 census. Of these, 1,139 lived in Co. Dublin with a further 462 living in Cork and 425 living in Antrim, virtually all of these in Belfast. Attesting to the nature of the British Empire at that time, and the high level of Irish service both in the military and civil service of India, the overwhelming majority of these persons were of British or Irish descent but had been born in India while their parents had lived and worked there. In total, it is possible to identify just three Indian nationals in the Irish census of 1911. These were Maneck Dalal, a twenty-seven-year-old medical doctor, listed as not practicing and who identified himself as a Zoroastrian; Kumaria Ayah, a forty-year-old Hindu children's nurse; and Coonoor Kinshnaswamy, a twenty-two-year-old Hindu, employed as nurse to a small boy and a domestic servant.[1] Interestingly, both servants identify themselves as being married for ten and two years respectively and it seems that their spouses were not in Ireland, suggesting that their migration arose out of economic necessity. It should be noted that 'ayah', listed as the name of Ms Kumaria Ayah above, is also the term applied to nannies and ladies' maids brought from Indian with returning British families during this period. Rozina Visram explains that ayahs were used as a form of cheap domestic labour at the time. They were also specifically employed as assistants to colonial families on the passage between Britain and India. With regard to domestic service, efforts were made in 1898 to establish a formal channel for the commercial importation of Indian domestic servants through the British government's India Office. This highlights the growing demand for Indian domestic servants at this time.[2]

Dublin was hardly as cosmopolitan as London or other major British urban centres of the early twentieth century. Census figures indicate that, although there were not insignificant numbers of French, German and Russian-born citizens in Dublin in 1911, foreign nationals from outside Europe were still a rarity in pre-First World War Dublin. While some insight into the social history of Ireland's Indians prior to 1913 can be garnered from Rozina Visram's in-depth study of the perception and reception of South-Asians in Britain stretching from the 1700s up to 1947, it is reasonable to assume that the Irish experience of distant migrant arrivals was quite different given the lack of pre-existing expatriate communities and networks such as existed in some of Britain's larger, and especially coastal, urban centres.[3]

Michael Kennedy records the existence of Dublin's first Indian restaurant which opened its doors for business in the summer of 1908, predating the opening of London's first twentieth-century Indian restaurant by three years. 'The Indian Restaurant and Tea Rooms' was located on Upper Sackville Street beside Dublin's iconic Gresham Hotel. Run by a Mr Karim Khan, the business struggled to make a commercial success and Kennedy reports that it had ceased trading within a year.[4] Ireland's small Indian community appears to have only established itself in the 1950s and it remained relatively small until at least the 1990s.[5] The most recent Irish census data (2011) shows 16,986 Indians living in Ireland: the seventh largest non-Irish ethnic group in the state.[6] Thus, in the context of a society with relatively low inward migration and persistent emigration from the middle of the nineteenth century until at least the middle of the twentieth, the arrival of groups of Indian law students, taking off as a phenomenon in 1913, constitutes an unusual influx. Their experience in Dublin would also be so.

V. V. Giri's journey to Dublin is, through his memoir, the best documented experience of travel from India to Dublin in 1913. He departed his hometown of Berhampur at the age of seventeen and spent a year studying English in Madras before he made his decision to travel to Britain and thence to Ireland. Departing in the spring of 1913, he travelled with his parents as far as Waltair and, from there, back to Madras alone. He then took boats to Dhanushkodi and onwards to Colombo where he boarded the S. S. Simla bound for England.[7] Giri observes that Colombo was the standard departure point for south Indians travelling to the United Kingdom at this time.[8] Antoinette Burton notes that it was often 'in the confined spaces of the railway carriage and the colonial cruise liner … that Indian students first encountered themselves as "othered" disjunctively in the eyes and reactions of the colonizer'.[9]

After a voyage, during which Giri recalls he suffered from seasickness and learned western table manners, he arrived in England and went to Tilbury, Essex. There, he stayed with a family friend, C. Sambasiva Rao, a fellow law student who had been three years in England at that point. Giri then moved to Talbot Road in Bayswater, London, where he says he spent four months 'acclimatising' himself.[10]

Linking in to the Indian community in London, Giri shared a room with a Hari Das, a Punjabi medical student. Giri notes that Das, with whom he remained friends, returned to India and joined the Indian Medical Service.[11] Giri also recounts how he met Gandhi in London at this point. He states that Gandhi was the one who advised the young Giri to abandon wearing his traditional Lal-imli suit and fez cap in preference for British attire.[12]

There are multiple explanations for why Giri chose to study in Dublin rather than London or another British city. The fact that Giri had hung around London for more than four months in 1913 suggests that he had not already decided to go to Dublin. Giri glosses over the background to this important decision in his autobiography stating that his father 'wanted me to join the Inns of Court [in London] and study law in England. Finally, it was agreed that I should go to the United Kingdom and join the National University of Ireland at the King's Inns, Dublin, as the first step towards becoming a Barrister.'[13] In his biography of Giri, G. S. Bhargava provides a little more detail on this decision, explaining how 'Giri set sail for the United Kingdom to qualify himself for the Bar. He took a fancy for the National University of Ireland and the King's Inns, Dublin.' He continues: 'When he decided to go to Ireland for his higher education Giri was not so much prompted by the affinity between our freedom struggle and the Irish urge for self-government as by the fact that there were many Andhra students studying there at the time. For a youth unused to the ways of western civilisation congenial company was naturally necessary under an alien sky.'[14] Supporting Bhargava's theory, of the twelve other pioneers in legal study who travelled on to Dublin in August 1913, seven of the eleven for whom place records can be traced were from the Andhra region.

These were not, however, the first students to have travelled from India to Dublin to study law. The very earliest Indian student in Dublin appears to have been Gnanam Dhanaswami Pillai, who entered TCD on 28 November 1905 and was registered as a student on 9 February 1906, listing his previous place of education as Madras University. He would be the first of many students coming from that city and underlining the strong educational ties between what is now Chennai and Dublin.[15]

After Pillai, the next identifiable Indian students arriving in Dublin are Javad Hussain of Saidapet, Madras and Bepin B. Verma of Shikanpore who began their studies at King's Inns in Michaelmas Term, 1912.[16] TCD also lists a number of Indian students, including three upon whom the degree of Bachelor in Laws was conferred in June 1912. However, these students do not appear in the rolls of the King's Inns nor are they on the university's membership lists in the previous year (1911–12), and they appear to have been pursuing an independent course of study.[17] Three further Indian students have been identified on the membership list of TCD for January 1913. These are Alam Mohammed Gadihuk and K. L. Kapur, two junior bachelors, along with one senior sophister, Satyendra Bhagat. As to what subjects these students were studying it is unclear.[18]

Indicating a level of institutional overlap, one of UCD's Indian students also appears in the Entrance Books of TCD. Brahmadesan Cidambi Sankara Narayana registered as a senior freshman at TCD on 23 January 1915 having previously begun the King's Inns approved law course at UCD in the autumn of 1914.[19] Evidently movement between the three institutions, UCD, TCD and the King's Inns, was fluid for Indians as members of Dublin's student community.

Giri's Classmates

In total, fifty Indian students studied law at UCD between 1914 and 1917. Giri was among UCD's first crop of thirteen students who appear in the UCD Calendar for 1914–15. Eleven of these had enrolled at the King's Inns in Michaelmas 1913 representing the first bulk entry of Indian students studying for the Bar there.[20] In the two following years, twenty-four and thirteen Indian law students enrolled at UCD, bringing the number to fifty. One of the 1916–17 class repeated in 1917–18 and one of the 1914–15 class appears to have repeated both in

1916–17 and again in 1917–18.[21] Although the attendance of Indian students at the King's Inns became a common, if not consistent, trend through the twentieth century, the influx of Indian students to UCD was a phenomenon of these years, evaporating to nothing by the conclusion of the First World War.

In terms of academic achievement, the Indian students not merely equalled their Irish classmates but several of them surpassed them conclusively. The UCD Academic Council minutes for 12 November 1915 record how Indian students swept up the top awards in the 1915 Law prizes. T. A. Chettiar came first in Jurisprudence, Constitutional Law and second in Roman Law to James G. O'Connor. Another Indian student, Syed Shah, topped the class in Law of Property and Contracts (Course B) as well as coming joint second in Jurisprudence behind Chettiar. Finally, in Constitutional Law, Daulat Ram Kalia came second to Chettiar. First place came with a prize of £3 in each instance whereas second place secured £2. In addition to all of the above, Chettiar was awarded the 1915 Dunbar Barton Prize for his overall marks in Law that year. The Dunbar Barton Prize came with a £10 cash stipend, meaning that Chettiar ended his 1915 examinations with £18 pounds in his pocket. The Dunbar Barton prize was awarded at the inaugural meeting of the 86th session of the King's Inns' Law Students' Debating Society on 21 October 1915. In awarding the prize to Chettiar, Mr Justice Barton commented that 'He knew of no better treatise in print than the treatise with which Mr. Chettiar had won this competition.'[22]

Among the Indians at UCD were a number of quite notable individuals who were already prominent in Indian legal or public life prior to coming to Ireland. Chief among these was Chettiar who was relatively older than his classmates. He was thirty-five when he entered the course as opposed to an average age among his Indian classmates of twenty-two and a half.[23] The eldest son of a M. R. Ry. T. Pattabirama

Chettiar Avergal of Salem, Madras, he came to Dublin with his wife and child.[24] Prior to his coming to Dublin, Chettiar had held several municipal and honorary positions in Madras including special magistrate, vice-president of the local board and honorary visitor of the Salem Gaol. A book catalogue from this period shows that, in 1905, Chettiar had published an article on the potential positive impact of Esperanto for India.[25] Chettiar should not be confused with the other more famous T. A. Ramalingam Chettiar who was also later a friend of V. V. Giri but two years younger than Chettiar the Dublin legal scholar. T. A. Ramalingam Chettiar became a leading figure in the Tamil Nadu cooperative movement and MP for Coimbatore in the Lok Sabha, 1951–52.[26]

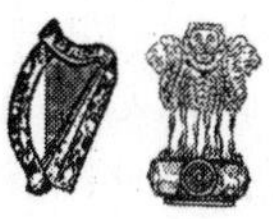

Chapter 4

Studying in a City in Turmoil: Lockout, War and Revolution

It is important to consider the social and political contexts of the city in which the first batch of Indian students found themselves in the late summer of 1913.Although viewed as a calm before the storm in British and western European history, the period August 1913 to August 1914 was one of intense turbulence in Irish history, much more so than after the outbreak of the First World War. In 1915, reflecting on the prelude to the First World War, Prime Minister Herbert Henry Asquith stated his belief that the outbreak of war in Europe 'could be seen as the greatest stroke of luck in his lucky career' as it had taken the focus and the heat off Ireland.[1]

In this tense Irish antebellum, Indian students were not immune from developments in Dublin. On 25 November 1913, a public meeting was held to inaugurate a paramilitary force, the Irish Volunteers, to defend the principle of Irish Home Rule. The founder and leader of the movement was UCD Professor of Early (including Mediaeval) Irish History, Eoin MacNeill. However, the UCD connections with the movement went much deeper than that. By February of 1914, the Irish Volunteers had established connections with some of UCD's Indian student body. On 7 February 1914, the first issue of a new newspaper entitled *The Irish Volunteer*, aimed specifically at the organisation's membership, was published. From then until the early months of the War, this paper became a popular and important forum for the rapidly expanding movement. In the fifth issue of the paper on 7 March 1914, the first of two articles entitled 'Indian Nationality: A Parallel with Ireland' appeared.[2] The mystery of the authorship of these pieces can be cleared up by reference to a letter from 1948 written to the former Taoiseach Éamon de Valera. The author of this letter, P. S. T. Sayee (Pangulury Sesha Thalpasaye), claims not only to have written these pieces but also to have '[undergone] training along with the Irish Volunteers in Dublin'.[3] Despite concerted efforts, both by Kate O'Malley and by myself in researching this book, no further evidence of Indian students parading with the Irish Volunteers has been uncovered. However, yet again, a tantalising lead into the interactions of Indian students and Irish rebels begs further illumination.[4]

The only surviving testimony of an Indian link with the Irish Volunteers comes from the Bureau of Military History (BMH). One witness, Seamus Ua Caomhánaigh, recalls his close friendship with one Indian student although he remembers this as dating from the War of Independence period, 1919–21. As Ua Caomhánaigh explains,

> During all this time I seldom slept at home. I got frequent orders from Mick Collins not to go home … On one of these occasions I went down to Adelaide Road to the house where a friend of mine, an Indian student at the University named Gupta, was in digs. He had frequently told me to come to him if hard pressed and he would put me up. It was rather late in the night when I got there and he had no time to make the arrangement he'd have liked, but he went into the room of another Indian chap, a friend of his, and gave his room to me.[5]

Given that the only Gupta who appears in the rolls of the King's Inns is Polisetty Hanumayya Gupta and he was called to the Bar on 18 January 1917 and he was already an established figure in the Indian independence struggle by 1921, it is possible that Ua Caomhánaigh misremembered the date and exact circumstances of this incident as it more likely occurred in the aftermath of the 1916 Rising.[6]

Returning to the articles which appeared in the *Irish Volunteer* in 1914, the pieces raise some interesting questions not only about their author but also about who commissioned them, and what they can tell us about the Irish Volunteers' perception of their movement in global and imperial contexts. In terms of understanding Giri and his contemporaries, the articles represent one of the very few surviving primary source documents which give an insight into the political outlook of these students while they were resident in Dublin.

An interesting editorial preface to the article explains that '[t]he following is contributed by an Indian Nationalist, who is amazed at the amount of liberty England permits in Ireland. No Indian is allowed to drill or carry a weapon.'[7] This comment exposes the mind-set of the paper's (Irish) editorial staff. It exhibits the obsession with firearms which had become such a dominant trait in this period when a new paramilitary vogue was sweeping both the nationalist and unionist community on the island. However, within the article, a different outlook is evident. Focussing on the issues of deportation without trial and the crime of sedition, the author employs both nationalist and anti-imperialist arguments to connect the Indian and Irish struggles. The author underlines how Indian nationalism is supressed in India through sedition legislation and cites the sympathetic Indian administrator Sir Herbert Risley in defence of this view. Risley had died in 1911 but, as a member of the council presided over by Lord Minto which had instituted a series of liberalising reforms for India in 1909, Risley had issued a sharp criticism of the old system of colonial governance of which he had been a part. Using Risley's definition of sedition, the author of 'Indian Nationality ...' wrote of how '[Risley] explained ... that what he meant by sedition in India, "that is to say that the Government is foreign, and, therefore, selfish, that it drains the country of its wealth, and has impoverished the people[,] that it allows Indians to be ill-treated in British colonies, that it levies heavy taxes on the people and spends them on the army, that it pays high salaries to the Englishmen and employs Indians in the worst paid posts" is sedition'.[8]

Risley was one of the foremost anthropologists and ethnographers of India, having published his four volume *The Tribes and Castes of Bengal* between 1891 and 1892. He was on the sympathetic wing of the British colonial administration of India and thus it would seem that the 'Indian Nationalist' writing in the *Irish Volunteer* was outlining a programme for reform rather than revolution. Lord Hardinge, who had been appointed Viceroy of India in 1910, comes in for criticism as the antithesis of Risley. To Sayee, Risley was 'posing as champion of India in far-away colonies while he has at heart the best interests of Britain un-doubtedly at the cost of India'.[9] Despite the rhetoric of reform, under Hardinge, policies such as deportation without trial and prosecution for sedition continued.

One of the most interesting Indo-Irish parallels to be explored in Sayee's article concerns the similarity of Irish experience with surrender and regrant and the more recent experiences of Indian chiefs. From the 1530s onwards, during the Tudor reign and conquest of Ireland, this policy brought Irish lords and chieftains under the jurisdiction of the British monarchy. Irish nobles relinquished their titles and were then bestowed with fresh title by the King. From 1541, this system was enhanced when Henry VIII of England became recognised as King – as opposed to Lord – of Ireland.[10] In the Indian case, Sayee explained:

> Besides oppressing the people that are directly under its control, it is unscrupulously going to the extent of invoking the help and co-operation of the Indian chiefs by method which were well known in Ireland in the past. The sight of the Government of India turning to Indian chiefs for help in restoring peace and order, as it understands them … brought forth an indignant protest from the leader writer of a Dublin daily newspaper which, perhaps, your readers may have seen.[11]

Sayee concluded with an appeal for solidarity and an almost prophetic vision of imperial collapse which would soon be visited not on the British, but on the German, the Austro-Hungarian, Russian and Ottoman empires. In this, he captures a zeitgeist of emerging anti-imperialism and nationalism which would echo down through the rest of the twentieth century in different parts of the world:

> My final appeal to all those that are interested in the well-being of humanity is to try and remove this crisis by the force of civilized opinion, since an Empire built on this sort of evil foundation, with all its destructive tendencies developed, and a delusive external appearance, must fall to pieces and involve world-wide disaster.[12]

Chapter 5

Subversion and Student Societies

By virtue of the secrecy it entailed, there are barely any traces of the views and activities of Indian students on either Irish or Indian political affairs. In his memoir, Giri includes a passage which every biographer dreads: 'On another occasion my diaries narrowly escaped discovery. Later I destroyed them myself and resolved to avoid this habit of introspection on paper, however commendable, I had been taught, it was.'[1] While Giri's personal destruction of his Irish diaries is a great disappointment to the historian, the fact that he destroyed them is significant in its own right and speaks to the high level of surveillance under which Indian students were placed in Britain and Ireland during these years.

What little we do know about this important aspect of Indian student experience in Ireland will be discussed in the next chapter. However, it is important first to discuss the aspects of Giri's time in Dublin for which concrete archival sources exist, namely his studies. From records in both the King's Inns and UCD, it is possible to reconstruct a relatively full picture of Giri and his Indian classmates. As with all student records, these constitute snapshots of the individual at examination and graduation. Points of contact with lecturers and tutors as well as a theoretical routine can be worked out but the lived experience of lectures, libraries and leisure remains occluded.

It is important to state that, despite the emphasis placed on UCD in his memoir, the primary purpose of Giri's coming to Ireland was to study at the King's Inns in Dublin. His engagement with the new National University was, in some respects, an unexpected afterthought and a decision that was made following his arrival in Dublin. After greater formalisation of legal training in the second half of the nineteenth century, students of the King's Inns attended terms of compulsory lectures and sat annual examinations while progressing through their studies. The number of terms which a student was required to attend at the King's Inns could be reduced if a student performed sufficiently well at exams, a privilege which was won by at least two Indian students, T. A. Chettiar and Daulat Ram Kalia, who were excused attendance for one term of lectures and one term of required dining at Commons on foot of their examination results in October 1916.[2]

The Law Students' Debating Society at the King's Inns was a vibrant part of student life there. For the session 1914–15, both Giri and his classmate Brahmadesam Cidambi Sankara Narayana were elected onto the committee of the society.[3] Under the auditorship of Bernard J. Fox, later County Court Judge for Antrim and Recorder of Belfast, their fellow committee members included James McSparran, future nationalist MP in Northern Ireland and chairman of the Anti-Partition League in the 1940s and 1950s; and Cecil P. Lavery who served as Irish Attorney General as well as a judge of the Irish Supreme Court, 1950–66.[4] Indicating their acceptance by their peers, Narayana and another Indian student, P. V. Gharpuray were elected the following year, this time elevated from ordinary committee members to secretary and treasurer respectively.[5]

While members of the student body seem to have accepted their Indian classmates readily, officialdom was less enthusiastic about embracing its new cohort of students, an attitude which, it will be seen, was common to UCD as well. In the minute book of the Benchers of the King's Inns, a number of Indian students can be found applying for entry to the King's Inns during the autumn and winter of 1913. A Mr F. A. Wyeysekera submitted a memorial to the Benchers of the King's Inns in October 1913 but this was unanimously refused.[6] A second student was denied entry after a vote on 1 November 1913. Although Indian students were entering successfully from as early as Michaelmas term 1912, the conditions of their entry remained ambiguous until early 1914 when the standing committee of the Benchers was ordered to consider the matter and instructed to report on the necessary alterations and additions to the rules of the society to meet these cases.[7] Although not minuted, the arrangement instituted on the advice of the standing committee appears to have been *ad hoc* rather than permanent because, by October of 1914, minutes begin to appear listing petitions and appeals from Indian students to have 'the present rules regarding admission' extended.[8]

By April of 1915, the Indian students had sought the intercession of the Student Department of the India Office in their defence. An official wrote to the Benchers of the King's Inns requesting that they 'extend the period of privileges to Indian students for admission till [sic] after the War.'[9] In response to this request, the Benchers refused to go beyond an earlier concession that the privileges would be extended to Michaelmas of 1915.[10] A petition for further extension in November 1915 was denied. However, in January 1916, on foot of a letter from the India Office, a *modus vivendi* was arrived at and some clarity given to the Indian students whose positions at the King's Inns were now in limbo. The Education Committee of the King's Inns recommended:

> That any student who entered the So
> before the new Code of Rules came i
> be permitted to complete his cou
> which was in operation at the date of his

At the following meeting, on 18 January 1916, this and other resolutions were adopted which finally gave clarity to the Indian students, more than two years after the vast majority of them had entered the Inns.[12]

Significantly, the minutes of meetings of the Benchers of the King's Inns give an unparalleled insight into the ways in which the First World War had an impact on the lives and studies of Indian students in Dublin. One might naturally assume – given the distances involved – that Indian students remained in Ireland and Britain throughout the course of their studies here. However, the Benchers' minutes paint a very different picture. On 9 June 1915, two students who had entered the Inns with Giri at Michaelmas 1913 requested credit for lectures they had missed in Michaelmas term of 1914 'owing to the difficulty in returning from India on the outbreak of the War'.[13] Earlier, in January 1915, another student, Bijay Narayan Agasti, had shown up in Dublin and was requesting admittance 'as, owning to the War he was unable to present himself in Michaelmas Term'.[14] Whereas Agasti's case is the earlier example, the really significant finding is that Indian students travelled back and forth to India during their time in Dublin. This raises the possibility that new ideas and attitudes were filtering home during these students' courses of studies in person, and not merely by correspondence. Moreover, it forces us to consider that the influence which students such as Giri had upon their return may have been predated in certain districts where Indian students were importing their newfound ideas as early as 1914 rather than 1916 as other evidence suggests.

The Benchers' minutes also reveal that at least one King's .nns student left Dublin for military duties during the war. Aftab Rai, who entered the Inns at Michaelmas 1914, was granted a memorial 'that he be given credit for his First Year, having passed the Final Examination in the subjects of the lectures he did not attend owing to absence from Dublin on Military Duties'.[15] Rai's medical card survives in the British National Archives but provides no information except that he was a member of the Indian Volunteer Ambulance Corps.[16] In a short article on Asians in British service during the first and second world wars, the British Library explains that Indian students, recruited by Gandhi, served in ambulance roles in Britain during the First World War where they tended to Indian war wounded at military hospitals, citing the converted Royal Pavilion in Brighton as one of the most notable sites in which Indian student medical orderlies served. Brighton accommodated over 600 Indian casualties from the western front.[17]

The role of Gandhi in raising ambulance volunteers for the crown forces dates back to the second Boer War in 1899. Upon the outbreak of the European conflict in 1914, Gandhi was in London and thus urged the Indian students of Britain to volunteer in what was officially titled the Field Ambulance Training Corps.[18] Whether through the appeal of Gandhi or not, it appears Rai travelled to Britain and became a part of this, most likely in the summer or autumn of 1915.[19] Interestingly, Aftab Rai was not one of the King's Inns students studying at UCD at this time. He does not appear in the annual university calendars for TCD either, suggesting that he may have fulfilled his requirements for study beyond the King's Inns curriculum at a British university. This may further explain his seemingly unique position serving as an ambulance volunteer in 1915 – something which, it will be seen, ceased to be unusual by April 1916.

Although Rai appears to have been the only one of Dublin's Indian students who actually joined the Field Ambulance for some party leaders, 'the war was looked upon as a useful means of propaganda for the attraction of new recruits'.[25] Furthermore, he wrote about how 'the individual power of the leader undergoes an immeasurable increase at a time when the majority of the members of all parties are under arms'.[26] In the cases of Gandhi and Redmond, even on the peripheries of the empire in India and Ireland, the war forced difficult policy decisions which proved controversial with followers. With reference to Giri, his apparent rejection of Gandhi's policy was mirrored by many younger and more radical Irish men and women who rejected Redmond's support for Britain. Many of these individuals ultimately ended up fighting their own battle at home in 1916.

Chapter 6

Teachers and Lectures

During their course of study at the King's Inns, students were required to attend one continuous and complete course (commencing in Michaelmas term) of three terms of lectures with a professor who lectured on 'Feudal and English Law, or the Law of Real Property, and a like course of one other of the Professors in the Law School of either Trinity College, Dublin, or University College, Dublin'.[1]

In the Annual Calendar for UCD the regulations for King's Inns students stipulated that students enrolling in one of the two universities based on the above were required to pass their requisite college exams to obtain credit for their first year at the Inns and progress into second and third year.[2]

At UCD, King's Inns students were required to attend Law of Property (course B) along with one of the following:

> Jurisprudence and International Law, Roman Law, or Constitutional History, Constitutional Law and Law of Evidence.[3]

In these subjects, the students would have encountered three very different individuals as their professors. The youngest of the three law professors at UCD was James Augustine Murnaghan. At the age of twenty-nine, he was appointed

Professor of Jurisprudence, Roman Law and International Law at UCD. His father George had been an Irish MP at Westminster until 1910 and James had been one of the committee which had drawn up the statutes of the National University that same year. By 1912, he was secretly advising the Irish Catholic hierarchy on the contents of the third Irish Home Rule Bill.[4] Arthur Clery was Professor of Law of Property. He was the most radically inclined of the three law professors. He was a member of the Irish Volunteers and, when that organisation split in the autumn of 1914, he sided with his UCD colleague, the historian Eoin MacNeill, staying with the rump of the Irish Volunteers and rejecting John Redmond's pro-war, pro-enlistment policy. Although he did not participate in the 1916 Rising, Clery was one of only two barristers who participated in the revolutionary Sinn Féin courts during the Irish War of Independence in 1920.[5]

Much more senior than his two colleagues, the most established and best known member of the Law faculty at the time was John Gordon Swift MacNeill. Since 1882, Swift MacNeill had been Professor of Constitutional and Criminal Law at the King's Inns. At UCD he became Professor of Constitutional Law and the Law of Public and Private Wrongs. More than twice the age of his junior colleagues, Swift MacNeill had been an MP for the constituency of Donegal South since 1887. Swift MacNeill appears to have been well liked by his Indian students and to have taken a special interest in them. As will be shown subsequently, when the Indian students faced real adversity in later years, Swift MacNeill offered a staunch defence of one of his students directly to the Prime Minister in the House of Commons.

Beyond the Law: Studying Arts at UCD

Whereas the majority of Indian law students in Dublin in this period appear to have focused on their legal studies, Giri was one of a number who resolved to study for a full BA degree course while in Dublin. Before even listing his law professors, Giri gives first prominence in his memoir to his arts degree course, listing his subjects as 'Literature, Economics and Political Science'. His lecturers in these subjects were Professor Robert Donovan and Thomas MacDonagh (English) and Rev. Fr Thomas A. Finlay (Political Economy).[6] Initially, these claims proved doubtful and seemingly impossible to substantiate from printed primary sources. No exam results are listed for Giri or any other Indian student under these subject categories nor does he or any of his fellow Indian law students appear on the membership lists for these classes. Only by going into the administrative records of UCD – the minute books of its Governing Authority and its Academic Council – is it possible to unearth the convoluted story of Indian student participation in the BA course at UCD.

The story begins with a minute for 8 October 1913 in which it is recorded:

> The application of five students of Madras University for admission to the college to study the full B.A. course was considered. It was decided to admit them provisionally to the classes and to ask the Board of Studies to consider Indian equivalents to matriculation.[7]

The note itself is crossed out and a marginal note beside it records that the question of Madras matriculation arose and the matter was postponed for further discussion.[8] Academic Council met regularly and conducted a large amount of university business but, for the following three months, there is no further mention of the topic until a minute of 29 January 1914. Here, it is simply recorded that 'The application of Mr Subba Row to attend courses in Arts was left in the hands of the President'.[9] Panguluri Venkata Subbarow was one of Giri's classmates in the Law School and a fellow Madras Presidency native, coming from Jammulapalem.[10] No record of the President's decision taken in Subbarow's case is recorded and no further word is given, either in the minutes of university meetings or in the printed university calendars until October 1914 when the Registrar of the University, Professor Arthur Conway, reported to Academic Council that 'two Indian students had presented themselves for lectures in Political Economy and English and it was ordered that they should be admitted'.[11] At the next day's Governing Body meeting, the Registrar reported the finding of Academic Council.[12] This appeared to finally give some clarity to the students involved. A further resolution later that month qualifies that, in the case of Indian student admissions, Academic Council would consider each application separately.[13]

Before a seemingly successful conclusion to the students' long battle for admission to UCD was reached, one Indian student took to UCD's student magazine, *The National Student* in June of 1914, to air his grievance. Of UCD, the anonymous student complained:

> Almost all English and Scottish Universities of any note recognise the Indian Universities and admit the Indians to the various arts and science courses without requiring them to take Latin and other classical languages. The National University ignores the existence of all the Indian Universities ... It expects even the Indian graduates to begin their A B C again in Ireland, along with Latin, if they wish to take a degree.[14]

Singling out UCD President Denis Coffey, to whom the ability to adjudicate over the Indian student's cases had been devolved, the article in the *National Student* explained:

> Some of the King's Inns students joined the National University, thinking that they would be permitted to

> attend the arts lectures and applied to the President for admission. The President was not pleased to give a reply to their petitions. The students came to know that their applications were either rejected or not considered at all.[15]

In absolving themselves of the duty of having to profess on these cases in their meetings, the Academic Council and Governing Body of UCD thus avoided having to minute the decisions that were made over the summer of 1914 into what seems to be a large number of Indian student petitions. Concluding his critique of the University's President and his administration, the student chastened his opponents:

> This is the treatment meted out to the Indian students by the National College where Mr Swift MacNeill, who is considered to be a political friend of India, is a professor and Mr [John] Dillon a member of the Governing Body.
>
> As regards Trinity College I have not much to say. If an Indian student wishes to enter its gates, in addition to English, he must learn two more foreign languages, Latin and French.[16]

Returning to the resolution of this impasse in October 1914, given that subjects listed in the minutes tally with what Giri recalls studying in his memoir, it can thus be taken that one of the two students who was successfully admitted on this occasion was Giri. It is, furthermore, likely that Subbarow was the other student given that he is named in a previous minute as wishing to study arts.

English

In his biography of Giri, S. R. Bakshi notes that, following his studies in Khallikote College High School, Giri went to

Madras to study under the Tamil writer M. S. Purnalingam Pillai, thus presumably placing Giri as a student in Madras Christian College where Purnalingam Pillai taught.[17] The author of several other works on Tamil literature and other topics, the frontispiece of Purnalingam Pillai's 1928 *Ravana the Great: King of Lanka*, identifies him as '*Emeritus Professor of English, Bishop Heber College, Trichinopoly, and Author of Tamil India, Ten Tamil Saints, etc.*'[18]

Significant in relation to Giri's time in Ireland, Bakshi notes that Pillai was a master in Shakespearian literature, an assertion borne out by the fact that he published in 1913, the year after Giri had studied with him, *Full Notes on A. T. Quiller Couch's Historical Tales from Shakespeare and Washington Irving's England's Rural Life and Christmas Customs.*[19] Giri lists English first among the subjects he studied in Dublin in his autobiography. He notes that he was lectured by Professor Robert Donovan and Thomas MacDonagh, Donovan's assistant lecturer. Donovan was, likewise, an avid Shakespeare enthusiast given its prominence in his teaching syllabus at UCD. The English syllabus which Giri would have studied saw him read *As You Like It, Hamlet, King Lear* and *Twelfth Night* as his 1915–16 Shakespearian texts under Professor Donovan.[20]

While Shakespeare provides an interesting bridge between Giri's teachers in India and Ireland, his tutor in English provides the closest confirmable link between Giri and the Irish Volunteers. Thomas MacDonagh had been appointed assistant lecturer in English at UCD in 1911 after having secured first class honours in his MA there. MacDonagh had previously been assistant headmaster at St Enda's college, the experimental progressive school established by Patrick Pearse at Ranelagh, in Dublin, in 1908. By 1913, Pearse and MacDonagh had both joined the newly founded Irish Volunteers. MacDonagh was a member of the provisional committee of this new paramilitary group and rose steadily through its ranks. By March of 1915, he was commandant of the Second Battalion of the Dublin Brigade, simultaneously being sworn in to the secret conspiratorial Irish Republican Brotherhood (IRB).[21] Pearse had been a member of the IRB since December 1913 and had, since October 1914, been part of a clandestine IRB committee investigating the feasibility of an Irish insurrection. In time, MacDonagh would also enter into this conspiracy.

MacDonagh's radical politics and his belief in physical force permeated into the classroom at UCD. By November 1915, the President of UCD was sufficiently concerned about MacDonagh's extracurricular military activities that he told the Under-Secretary for Ireland, Matthew Nathan, that 'He [MacDonagh] would try to take an opportunity of talking with students.'[22] Austin Clarke was a fellow student of MacDonagh's. Years later, he recalled how, by the spring of 1916, MacDonagh began to look 'abstracted and worried' in class. Clarke goes on to recall how, 'one day, during a lecture on the Young Ireland Poets, he took a large revolver from his pocket and laid it on the desk, "Ireland can only win freedom by force" he remarked, as if to himself.'[23] Clarke was studying for an MA in 1916, and would go on to replace MacDonagh as assistant lecturer in English after the latter's execution. Although Giri would thus not have been in the same class as Clarke, this anecdote gives further insight into the nature of MacDonagh's classes at UCD which one student remarked were 'never relevant and invariably interesting.'[24] As a point of contact between militant Irish republicanism and Giri, MacDonagh provides the strongest link. It will be shown subsequently how Giri emphasised the influence which his young lecturer had on him when he met Irish diplomats in his later years as president.

Political Economy

If MacDonagh instilled nationalist radicalism into Giri as a student, then his other chosen arts subject likewise put him in contact with one of the university's great exponents of social reform, Thomas Aloysius Finlay. Finlay, a Jesuit priest, was Professor of Political Economy at UCD. Finlay had been impressed by the reformist agricultural policies of the Prussian government when he was abroad as a student, something he applied upon his return home through his involvement in the agricultural co-operation movement in Ireland. Fellow reformer and co-operative champion Sir Horace Plunkett said of Finlay that he had, 'for a full half-century, laboured disinterestedly for the moral, social, and economic uplifting of the Irish poor'.[25] Between the influence of MacDonagh and Finlay, it is clear Giri was immersed in a culture of education that stressed self-sacrifice, vocationalism and volunteering.

Studying political economy in UCD consisted, in the first year, of three lectures per week on 'a general treatment of the subjects ... with a brief study of International Trade and Taxation'.[26] Second-year students studied the following subjects:

- Fundamental Notions: economics, wealth, value, price, etc. Production: land, labour, organisation of labour, capital, growth of capital, progress, growth of population, development of industrial and commercial organisation, limitations and checks.
- Consumption: place in economic theory, marginal values, reaction of consumption on production.
- Exchange: barter, sale, market price, relation of market price to cost of production, money and its functions, value of money, coinage, single and double standards, credit, various forms of credit, the currency, banking.

- Distribution: property, communism and socialism, property in land, rent, peasant proprietors, other forms of land tenure, wages, wages fund, rates of wages, trade unions, unemployment, profits, rates of profit, combination of capitalists, the entrepreneur, interest.[27]

Given the importance labour relations would take in Giri's subsequent career, it is likely that Finlay's lectures played no small part in shaping Giri's views; especially his lectures on production and distribution. Thus, just as with nationalist thought, there was a synergy between what Giri was experiencing in the classroom and what he was witnessing on the streets of Dublin both during the 1913 Lockout and in the prelude to the 1916 Rising. If one is looking for a *Bildungsroman* of the future president, the lectures he attended in Dublin were formative experiences.

Perceptions of Indian Classmates among Irish Students

Among Giri's classmates at the King's Inns were several figures who would later rise to prominence in the Irish judiciary. Arguably his best-known classmate, both at King's Inns and at UCD, was Cahir Davitt, second son of the celebrated radical nationalist and agrarian socialist Michael Davitt. Davitt was appointed the first Judge Advocate General of the National Army during Ireland's Civil War in August 1922. Davitt's other major contribution during the period of state formation came when he was appointed to the judiciary committee which advised the Free State government on the establishment of the courts system in 1923–24. He concluded his military duties in 1926 and served as a circuit court judge before being appointed to the Irish High Court in 1945. He became president of the High Court in 1951, a role he held until his retirement in 1966.[28]

Davitt entered the King's Inns at Michaelmas 1913 just like Giri. He had already been studying for a BA at UCD which he was awarded in 1914 before going on to study for an LLB at UCD simultaneous to his King's Inns studies. During his student days at UCD and the King's Inns, Davitt knew many of the Indian students. At the King's Inns' junior class continuous course examination in 1915, twenty-three of the fifty-four students sitting the exam with Davitt were Indians, with Giri among them.[29] Davitt was among just five students to be called to the Bar on 18 January 1916. With him on that day was one Indian student, Giri's former housemate, Shri Unnava Lakshminarayana, of whom more will be said later.[30]

It is difficult to gauge the reception of Indian law students by their Irish classmates as little written evidence of their friendships and encounters survives. However, this is not extraordinary. Very little of any substance, such as letters or diaries, survives to document the interrelations of Irish students with other Irish students either.[31] For the most part, it is necessary to rely on memoirs to reconstruct the social networks of students and, while Giri remembers much of his lecturers and professors, he provides very little detail on his Irish classmates. Likewise, the Irish student memoirs consulted have virtually nothing to say about Indian classmates.[32]

One quite unique document exists which gives some sense of the perception of Indian students amongst their classmates. In the December 1915 edition of the *National Student*, a poem, entitled 'Indian Nights' Entertainments', gives a satirical account of some of the Indian students at UCD. Apart from its questionable rhyme and metre, it is difficult to discern the tone of the piece and to ascertain whether it signifies acceptance or derision of the students mentioned. Given the other evidence pointing to the inclusion of Indian students in various aspects of student life, and Giri's highly positive memories of Ireland in his autobiography, the latter seems more likely. It is hard to know how seriously the Indian students took themselves and how such verse would have been received. It should be noted that Irish students, including Cahir Davitt, were similarly teased in verse in the *National Student*, suggesting this was a ritual light-hearted and friendly activity among students. The three stanzas of the poem which name individual students go as follows:

I.
There was a young fellow called Chettyar
Who said 'What a dandified settyar.
'The hats you have here
'Are damnably dear,
'And really a turban is prettyar'.

II.
That zealous Hindoo Narrayana
Learned Irish from Mr. Sean Breathnach.
He stuck him one day
When he said, 'Tell me pray
'The Irish for Have a banneathnach'.

III.
An Excellent fellow called Giri
Once wended his way into Niri.
When satiety urged
He slowly emerged,
And his gait was decidedly biri.[33]

This irreverent composition was signed off with the pseudonym Robin Mac Tagore, a mock Gaelicisation of Rabindranath Tagore, reflecting Irish students' recollections of Tagore three years after his visit to Dublin with Yeats. The poem indicates those aspects of the Indian students which Irish students found most exotic or interesting: dress and deportment, Indian interest in the Irish language and, in Giri's case, the culture clash of Indian values and the Irish public house. 'Niri' refers to Neary's pub on Chatham Street in Dublin. It is impossible to know if Giri frequented the establishment, although his conscientiousness about his vegetarianism while in Dublin and his involvement in the picketing of shops selling alcohol upon his return to India suggest he was strict in his observance of Indian cultural practices during his time in Ireland.[34]

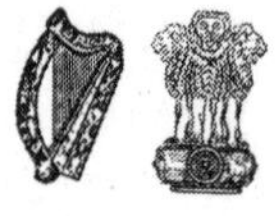

Chapter 7

Student Politics: Indian Activism and Radical Irish Connections

Giri tells how he was 'drawn irresistibly into the cross currents of the Irish struggle for self-government' when he arrived in Dublin in 1913.[1] However, he was also mindful of the political situation he had left behind and remained active in Indian political activism during his time in Dublin. With the backdrop of a city that was going through its largest ever labour dispute and which was witnessing the formation of a paramilitary nationalist organisation, Giri was not short of patriotic or socially progressive inspiration during the winter of 1913–14. Dublin's new Indian students organised themselves into both open and secret societies around this time.

Giri and some other Indians were members of a small secret group calling itself the 'Anarchical Society'. Giri explains: 'We professed belief in using violence and bloodshed to achieve a peaceful end and started learning the techniques of incendiarism and bomb-making to help us in the freedom struggle on our return to India.'[2] Alex Tickell has observed that travel to Britain [and Ireland] as well as increased connectivity between the Imperial centre and the Indian periphery 'allowed Indian nationalists to enter into a cross-national dialogue with ... other anti-colonial groups (notably in Ireland and Egypt)'. Tickell emphasises how these developments exposed Indian nationalists to 'new terrorist strategies developed by [Irish] Fenian groups and anarchists ... tactics such as assassination and bombing which Indian activists euphemistically termed "Russian methods"'.[3]

A glance at the UCD student calendars suggests that the students would not have had to look as far as the Fenian underground for information on these topics in Dublin. These subjects were also popular among Irish students at a time when an open nationalist paramilitary organisation – the Irish Volunteers – was being established. The first lecture in the 1913–14 session of the UCD Engineering society was 'Use of explosives for Engineering purposes' by a Mr M. Dalton. Without casting a cynical eye on the scholarly earnestness of a student society, one might wonder if 'Engineering purposes' were in the mind either of Mr Dalton or of his audience given the contemporary political context.

Again, in the following academic year, with the First World War then underway, January 1915 saw the UCD Chemistry Society host a lecture given by M. J. Walsh, B.Sc., simply titled 'Explosives'.[4] Furthermore, the *Irish Volunteer* newspaper contained engineering notes and descriptive and explanatory articles on weaponry written by Laurence J. Kettle, brother of Thomas, Professor of National Economics at UCD.[5]

Giri claims that the leader of this 'Anarchical Society' was Shri Unnava Lakshminarayana. Lakshminarayana entered the King's Inns at the same time as Giri and he was from Guntur in Madras, not far from Giri's place of birth. Giri describes Lakshminarayana as an 'elderly gentleman' and 'the leader of the Indian student community'. Records for the King's Inns show that Lakshminarayana was thirty-three years old when he began his studies at the King's Inns. Giri, by contrast, had just turned nineteen. Lakshminarayana went on to become a poet and novelist. Velcheru Narayana Rao cites Lakshminarayana as being typical of a number of Indian students who returned from Britain and Ireland influenced by the Russian revolution. Rao notes that in Lakshminarayana's novel, *Mālapalli*, written in 1922–23, the plot centres on untouchables with Bolshevik ideas incorporated into it. Written while Lakshminarayana was in jail, the book was proscribed by the British authorities until 1928.[6] It is worth considering if what Rao identifies as Russian Bolshevism may in fact be the product of his Irish experiences, especially given that Lakshminarayana had finished his studies in Dublin in January 1916, although this did not necessarily mean he left immediately.

Most interesting of all is the fact that Giri shared a house with Lakshminarayana when he first moved to Dublin. Moving residence was an extremely common occurrence among Indian students in Dublin at this time. This is evidenced by the frequent crossing-out and re-entry of new addresses in the register of the King's Inns' Law Students' Debating Society.[7] Along with at least two other Indian students – Nadimpalli Dasaratha Ramayya and Kapally Ghantamraju – the four lived at 1 Grove Park, Rathmines.[8] All were from the Madras Presidency, two from Guntur, and the other from Krishna district. The house, the end of a long terrace, still stands to this day and is located directly beside the bank of Dublin's Grand Canal. The property's rear windows face directly onto the northern gate of Portobello Barracks, less than fifty metres beyond. The barracks was and is a key strategic military barracks in the city.[9]

Even before the year 1914 was out, both Giri and Lakshminarayana had moved to new residences. However, it is significant that the pair had lodged together in this early phase, suggesting this small unassuming house over the wall from a key British army barracks was a site in which these students discussed explosives and arson. Giri claims that the society changed direction when it came under the influence of Gandhi. Following this, the students decided 'to follow only the path of truth and non-violence for winning political freedom'.[10]

Thus, the closed, secret and violent society gave way to an open, or at least partially open, society named the Indian Students' Association of which Giri was secretary for three years.[11] While the students renounced violence, they appear to have become more active in their work for Indian freedom through this Association. The semi-secret work of this society was to propagate the ideas of non-violence and to expose British mis-rule of India. Giri describes a pamphlet which the society had printed in Dublin and claims 100,000 copies were made. He recalls its title as 'Horrors in South Africa' which seems to put beyond doubt that this is one and the same as 'South African Horrors: Drama in Five Scenes' a two-page printed pamphlet, in English, with pictures and stories of atrocities as listed on the South Asia Microform Project.[12]

In Giri's own words, the pamphlet aimed to 'magnify acts of racial discrimination perpetuated on the Indian community and their struggle against the White Minority Government [of South Africa]'.[13] He also notes that the pamphlet advocated passive resistance along the lines of Gandhi's philosophy. The pamphlet was intercepted by Customs and, in the inquiry that followed, it was traced back to its Dublin printer. This prompted a raid on Giri's lodgings but not before he had been tipped off by the printer and had time to destroy any evidence linking him to the pamphlet. Giri attributes the intervention of this printer, '[who was] a nationalist himself' as having saved him from arrest and deportation.[14]

The Politics of the Plate

In searching for routes of entry for Indian students into Irish radical politics, it is perhaps the dinner table as much as the lecture theatre that provided them with introductions. Akhila Jagdish, the great-granddaughter of V. V. Giri wrote how Giri fondly recollected his living arrangements in Dublin and that his landlady made special arrangements to cater for her Indian boarders and their vegetarian dietary requirements. She recounted how 'my great grandfather had rented a flat in Dublin. The landlady and her daughter had taken a shine to him and, every day, knowing that he was a vegetarian, would leave a cup of tea and biscuits for him, knowing that would be possibly the only meal he would have for the day.'[15]

Vegetarianism and politics are an unlikely meeting point when studying Indians in 1914 Dublin but it should be noted that at least one vegetarian restaurant was operating in Dublin during this period and it is reasonable to assume that Indian students sought it out when looking for suitable dining in the city. Located north of the river Liffey at number 21 Henry Street, the Irish Farm Produce Café was a shop and restaurant specialising in Irish-made produce and with a vegetarian restaurant also operating on the premises.[16] It was managed and run by Jennie Wyse Power. She was a feminist and nationalist who had been active in advanced politics since the days of the Ladies' Land League during the agrarian agitation of 1879–82. Subsequent to her involvement in this organisation, she had maintained an active role in Irish nationalist politics. She was a leading campaigner in the first Sinn Féin by-election in North Leitrim in 1908. By 1914, she was a veteran of radical politics. Her restaurant secured its place in the annals of Irish history when, in April 1916, seven members of the revolutionary Irish Republican Brotherhood assembled there to sign the proclamation that would be read to announce the establishment of an Irish Republic on Easter Monday 1916.

In 1922, the shop secured its place in literary as well as political history with the publication of James Joyce's *Ulysses* in which it is referenced as 'that Irish farm dairy shop John Wyse Nolan's wife has in Henry Street'. In the book, the fictional protagonist, Leopold Bloom, emerges from the shop with a jug of freshly purchased cream.[17] Before the 1916 Rising, Wyse Power's restaurant provided common ground where a range of individuals and groups holding advanced views on labour, suffrage and nationalism could meet and talk.[18] From 1914, adverts for the Irish Farm Produce Café appear in *An Claidheamh Soluis* (The Sword of Light), the official newspaper of the Gaelic League. The paper's management had been taken over by Michael Joseph O'Rahilly, better known as 'The O'Rahilly', in November 1913. Thereafter, the paper's content became much more politicised, aligning with the Irish Volunteers and other advanced nationalist causes with which O'Rahilly was associated.[19]

Although it is not possible to establish who exactly frequented Wyse Power's restaurant, it seems likely that it would have been a welcome place for Indian students, especially those like Giri who were interested in radical politics. Wyse Power had joined Inghínídhe na hÉireann (the Daughters of Ireland) in 1908 through the encouragement of her friend Helena Molony. It is likely, therefore, that she would have played a part in the Irish solidarity campaign for Dhingra when Molony took up this cause in her paper, *Bean na hÉireann*, the following year. The link between Wyse Power and Molony only serves to increase the likelihood that the Irish Farm Produce Café was a site of encounter for Irish advanced nationalists and Indian students in Dublin.

One customer who we know frequented the restaurant was Giri's English tutor, Thomas MacDonagh. A police intelligence file notes his entering the restaurant with 'two other Sinn Feiners'[20] on Tuesday 28 March 1916, less than a month before the outbreak of the insurrection on 24 April. However, the police informer, codenamed 'Chalk', believed that it was not vegetarian fare MacDonagh was after. MacDonagh and his associate were carrying 'heavy handbags which they left inside. It is believed that the bags contained ammunition.'[21] If this police informant is to be believed, Wyse Power's shop was being used as an ammunition dump in the immediate prelude to the Rising.

Chapter 8

1916: Suspicion and Sedition

By 1916, Indian students were well integrated into both student and city life in Dublin. Some had found common cause with the Irish Volunteers and participated enthusiastically in student societies. They even travelled around the rest of Ireland in spite of the restrictions imposed by the First World War.

In his biography of the future president, G. S. Bhargava notes that Giri made a visit to the southern Irish city of Cork in 1915. It is difficult to substantiate or deny this tale. The fact that it does not feature in Giri's own recollections of Ireland raises suspicions but, with caveats entered, it is sufficiently amusing to warrant retelling. The story dates to 1915, when Irish troops were heavily engaged against Ottoman forces in the Gallipoli campaign. Meanwhile in Cork, Giri had travelled down from Dublin as a tourist and, while making his way around the city, was apparently mistaken for a Turk on account of a fez cap he was wearing. Fearing that he was monitoring ships of the Royal Navy docked in the port city, Bhargava claims that police arrested Giri.[1] Apparently satisfied with his explanation that he was a student from Dublin on a bona fide sightseeing trip, he was released without charge.[2]

While the overzealousness of the Royal Irish Constabulary offers some comic relief to Giri's experiences with British and Irish officialdom, the more serious threat was posed by agents of the India Office who operated both inside the realm and beyond to conduct surveillance on, and operations against, Indian political radicals.[3] Indian Political Intelligence certainly appears to have kept tabs on Indian students in Ireland as much as they did on Indian students in Britain. However, outside the activities of police and agents of the India Office, there is no evidence to suggest that Indian students in Ireland were treated with suspicion on political grounds by members of the general public. For the state's part, episodes such as the Wyllie assassination served only to fuel the pre-existing tensions and suspicions of Indian students first formally confronted by the 1907 Lee-Warner Committee.[4]

Writing in the *National Student* prior to the outbreak of the war, an anonymous Indian student praised the general attitude of the Irish public in the course of his lament over the previously discussed administrative hurdles which were being placed in the way of Indian students. Of the Irish public, the author stated: 'the land of Burke and Sheridan was expected to be more sympathetic to her Aryan brethren from India. The people at large and the professors of the Universities are no doubt very sympathetic.'[5]

Despite this prevailing attitude of cosmopolitan tolerance, there is a sense that attitudes to non-nationals, of whatever origin, were hardening by the beginning of 1916. This was contributed to in no small part by the new phenomenon of the 'conscription exile': men of military age who travelled to Ireland following the passage of the Military Service Act in January 1916 in Britain. This may or may not be a factor in explaining the following, but one stark example of anti-Indian xenophobia has been identified, dating from the spring of 1916. A Dublin newspaper of questionable repute sprang up at this time and began to publish, among other scandalous content, racist articles against Dublin's Indian community. Although this newspaper's content might induce one to dismiss it as the unpopular ravings of a crank journalist, the fact that police intelligence reports record its print-run at 10,000 copies per week, demonstrates this was certainly not a marginal publication.[6] A short-lived venture, the history of the paper's demise is intimately linked with that of the Dublin insurrection which broke out on 24 April 1916. By digging deeper into this episode, some fascinating links between this instance of racism and one of the most infamous atrocities committed during the 1916 Rising have been established. It also draws the story of Dublin's Indian students into one of the mysteries of the 1916 Rising in a highly unexpected manner.

During the First World War, the Defence of the Realm Act and a strict culture of press censorship led to the rise of what has been dubbed the 'mosquito press'. No sooner was one paper shut down by the authorities than a new one sprang up. Editors and newspaper owners became increasingly innovative at finding ways to get around the censor. The best example was Arthur Griffith's short-lived newspaper, *Scissors and Paste*, which took excerpts from foreign and other newspapers which had already passed the censor and juxtaposed them in new ways in order to convey a different message.[7] Amid this new proliferation of the press, a new and highly unusual newspaper emerged in March of 1916. Entitled the *Eye-Opener*, there is perhaps no other paper from this era quite like it.

The *Eye-Opener* published threats more than stories. Its editor offered cash rewards to members of the public for tip-offs on scandals around the city of Dublin. In a city rife with political and radical press publications, it is difficult to classify the *Eye-Opener*. It is somewhere between a libellous gossip sheet and an organ of Dublin moral vigilantism. To quote one Dublin Castle official, it was 'a blackmailing production of the worst type'.[8] In its vigilantism, the paper provides a Dublin example of what the historian John Borgonovo has noted in relation to Cork city where the influx of thousands of American sailors in the summer of 1917 resulted in 'vigilance committees', encouraged by local clergy as well as local politicians.[9] As Borgonovo explains, these 'moral panics' were not purely a phenomenon of the First World War. Vigilance committees existed as far back as 1911 focussing on the censorship of certain literature. However, with the influx of soldiers and others, including refugees, during the war, moral vigilance patrols took on a more xenophobic slant. This surfaced not only in the case of anti-Indian sentiments as will be documented here but especially anti-British and later anti-American feeling among urban populations in Ireland. However, it should be noted that other wartime factors, such as the rise in prostitution around ports and barracks, meant that moral vigilance was as much a phenomenon of wartime Britain as it was of Ireland.[10] In Ireland, however, the campaigns were sometimes taken advantage of by advanced nationalists who harnessed moral panic and fears over the associations between Irish women and girls with soldiers and sailors to progress their own agendas of opposing recruitment and promoting anti-government sentiment.[11] In Cork in 1917, this had taken the form of large crowds carrying out verbal and even physical assaults on American sailors consorting with local women.[12]

Returning to the *Eye-Opener*, the paper's editor was one Thomas Dickson. Dickson has been described by some of those who encountered him in Dublin in this period as a disreputable and dislikeable character. The historian and journalist Frank McNally observes how Dickson was frequently remembered as being 'unsavoury'.[13] Michael Noyk, republican activist and legal advisor to Arthur Griffith, described Dickson in the following terms: 'There was at this period a very unsavoury gentleman in Dublin, a Scotsman named Dickson, who wrote a blackmailing paper called "The Eye-opener"."[14]

The paper published numerous tales of extra-marital affairs as well as articles of an anti-semetic and anti-English nature. One of its allegations centred on the rector of the Church of Ireland (Anglican) Holy Trinity Church in Rathmines, Dublin, a Reverend Ernest H. Lewis-Crosby.[15] The accusations made against the rector were sufficiently serious that his solicitor wrote to the Under-Secretary, Sir Matthew Nathan, at Dublin Castle, on 29 March 1916 to seek the suppression of the paper.[16]

On 18 March, in its third issue, the *Eye-Opener* targeted Dublin's Indian student community for the first time. Behind the racist overtones of this very short article – which includes references to these men as 'the Black Peril' and 'vampires' – are some interesting details about the prejudices and fears of the author. Echoing the concerns over moral rather than political panic which had spurred the British government to convene the Lee-Warner Committee in 1907, the *Eye-Opener* suggestively posited that Indian students were associating with Irish women. Explaining that 'We hear some rather startling tales about some of [the "coloured gentlemen" now residing in the city]', the paper continued: 'Some of the landladies in whose houses some of these gentlemen resided have had to eject them because of their disgraceful conduct.'[17]

In the following issue, published on 25 March, an anonymous female correspondent residing in the southern Dublin suburb of Dundrum wrote:

> I feel I must write and let you know of a certain young girl, not more than 19, whose father keeps a butcher shop in Parnell Street. I am sure her father is ignorant of the fact that she is very often in the company of these fellows, who, I am sure, mean no good.[18]

The author concluded her condemnation of this butcher's daughter by asserting that 'She is only one of many, which is a disgrace to the white race.'[19] For the editor of the paper, the letter was lauded because 'the words … used are sufficient in themselves to convey to our readers the fact that such a thing does exist in our midst as the Black Peril.'[20] Interestingly, these sentiments resonate closely with those of a Cork priest in September 1917 who provoked the ire of US Navy officers attending his sermon when he labelled the US sailors stationed in Cork 'vultures … who were preying upon the purity of our daughters …'[21]

The paper had drawn a mixed reaction to its campaign against Indians in Dublin city. In the same issue, it published a letter from 'A Coloured Gentleman' who objected to the fact that the *Eye-Opener* had labelled all such persons as the same. Seeking equal treatment with Irishmen, the author requested that the paper 'kindly address those coloured gentlemen individually in your paper, as you do with most of the Irish.' Interestingly, the correspondent concluded with an offer to provide 'any information about the men of disagreeable conduct in order to correct them.'[22] In an editorial comment classic of the faux egalitarianism which permeates the *Eye-Opener*, the editor explained that 'It is not the intention of the proprietors of this newspaper to hurt the feelings of any person. Our aim is simply to stamp out the vice that infests our city … We can assure the writer of the above letter that on the face of the globe there is not to be found a more homely or kindly people than the Irish, who always give to strangers a caed mile failthe [sic].'[23] Returning from platitudes to the soapbox of moral vigilantism, Dickson concluded that the paper would co-operate 'in clearing the city of Dublin of the presence of the gentlemen we referred to.'[24]

In the following issue, 1 April 1916, alongside articles against a Jewish draper, a portrait painting Belgian refugee, and a 'Phibsboro' Flapper', the paper again targeted Dublin's

Indian students.[25] However, by this point, Dublin's Indian students had resolved to complain to a higher authority about the racist columns of the *Eye-Opener*. A student living at the Kilworth Hotel on Kildare Street listed as a Mr S. M. Azam – the name does not appear in the TCD, UCD or King's Inns lists – complained to the Dublin Metropolitan Police on 30 March 1916 about the publication of the 'Black Peril' articles in the *Eye-Opener*. Following the paper's publication, the student reported 'that Indian Students were insulted in the streets by "Black Peril" being shouted after them.'[26]

Subsequent to Azam's complaint, Giri's classmates, B. N. Mahant, writing from the King's Inns, and D. R. Kalia, then resident at 21 Synge Street, addressed letters of grievance about the paper to the Lord Lieutenant of Ireland's Private Secretary. Kalia's letter contains much the same sentiments as the anonymously published letter, purporting to be from an Indian, published in the 25 March issue of the *Eye-Opener*. In the course of his long letter, Kalia states that 'The editor may have his motives, but … he should refrain from using language which exiles a community as a whole. Who would on earth think that every meeting of a coloured gentleman and a white lady is for immoral purposes? Does the editor want that there should be no social intercourse between two classes of His Majesty's subjects?'[27] The letter from B. N. Mahant, likewise, called for equal rights among Imperial subjects. Mahant reminded the Lord Lieutenant that 'During the war such a wretched publication can easily be stopped under the Defence of the Realm Act for inciting race hatred and disturbing peace.'[28]

Action from the authorities was swift. Police visited the printers of the *Eye-Opener*, Messrs Flynn and O'Brien, on the morning of 6 April. With only one side of the forthcoming issue printed, the printer agreed to cease publication immediately and not to print the title in future. A visit to the editor, Mr Dickson, that evening, however, was less successful.

The Dublin Metropolitan Police (DMP) report records that Dickson remained obdurate, telling the attending sergeant 'I take full responsibility as owner and publisher, I have published nothing scurrilous about anybody.'[29]

Following this action by police, and the refusal by Messrs Flynn and O'Brien to print the *Eye-Opener* on 6 April, developments gathered pace. On 12 April 1916, Dickson reappeared in court to answer a charge of criminal libel initiated by Joseph Isaacs, a businessman, Dublin Corporation member and, as was claimed at the hearing, the former landlord of Dickson to whom the latter was in arrears amounting to £40. Isaacs had, for weeks, been the subject of defamatory articles in the *Eye-Opener* including much content of a strongly anti-Semitic nature.[30] With this case ongoing, Dickson managed to get the paper back up and running with a new firm, the Dublin Printing Works, on Dublin's South King Street. Reduced from eight to four pages, the paper re-appeared on 15 April 1916 after a fortnight's hiatus.[31] Avoiding all but the most oblique reference to its previous attacks on Indian students, the paper carried much the same type of content as before. It also published Dickson's own account of the DMP's interventions leading to the halting of presses on 6 April.[32]

In spite of the paper's reappearance, and seemingly satisfied by the response of the authorities, a committee of Indian students was specially convened on 17 April in order to express a motion of thanks to the Lord Lieutenant. Presided over by Giri's classmate, Abdur Razzaq, the assembled students acknowledged the role played by the Lord Lieutenant in protecting Indians from 'scurrilous attacks'. A resolution was drawn up. It was respectively proposed and seconded by B. N. Agasti and J. N. Mahant, both of whom entered UCD Law the year after Giri. The resolution recorded:

> … our heartfelt gratitude to H. E. the Lord Lieutenant of Ireland for his so kindly expressing his sympathy with the

> Indian students and for the action he has so graciously taken in warning the owners, publishers, & printers of the *Eye-Opener* and thus protecting the Indians from the scurrilous attacks.[33]

The only other meeting of Indian students which is recalled as having happened at this point was of a very different nature. Referring to the close rapport he had with members involved in planning the 1916 Rising, Giri recalls in his memoir that 'about a week before the uprising we met some leaders of the movement. Desmond FitzGerald who was to become a minister of Government later actually said, "well, let us meet again at Easter for some hot tea."'[34] This story is corroborated by the fact that another student, P. S. T. Sayee, wrote to Éamon de Valera in 1948 recalling his time in Ireland. As Kate O'Malley records in *Ireland, India, and Empire*, Sayee claimed to de Valera that:

> I was intimately associated with your National Leaders of those glorious days … After the Rebellion of 1916 it became impossible for me to continue to stay in Dublin. I therefore left for Bray along with Mr Desmond FitzGerald and his family. After some time he [FitzGerald] was arrested and taken away and I found my way somehow back to India.[35]

A detailed search of Desmond FitzGerald's papers sheds no further light on Sayee's link with the FitzGerald household. Likewise, Kate O'Malley wrote to Desmond's son Garret while the latter was still alive and was told that there was no recollection of Sayee in the family. It should be remembered that FitzGerald's papers are comparatively scant in material relating to the 1916 period and that Garret FitzGerald was born in 1926 so, although nonetheless shaky, the absence of written evidence does not automatically mean that Sayee's recollection is inaccurate.[36]

On Wednesday 19 April 1916, the same day the above resolution was sent to the Lord Lieutenant, Dickson reappeared in court where the case for criminal libel was sent forward for trial. Dickson's bail was set at £30 with a further £30 security.[37]

Seemingly undeterred, that Saturday, 22 April, the *Eye-Opener* reappeared in Dublin newsagents as a full eight page paper. In stark defiance both of the legal proceedings against him and the warning regarding attacks on Indian students, Dickson held no punches in what he published. A summary of the proceedings against him was printed on page 2 while the letters column included one pertaining to the Indian students.[38] Purporting to come from 'Law Student, K[ing's]. I[nns]' with name and address enclosed, the letter represents perhaps the most damaging personal attack on an individual Indian student to have appeared in the paper. While there is no way of knowing whether this was indeed a genuine King's Inns student or merely the vitriol of Dickson himself, the details of the letter indicate that it was referring to a specific Indian student in Dublin and that the level of detail given would have made his identity relatively clear to his friends and neighbours.

The anonymous author proceeded to link in with the moral crusade then being waged in the *Eye-Opener*, commending the editor on 'opening the eyes of the public to the sins of the monsters who in human shape, acting as agents of hell, go about seeking whom they may scandalise and destroy'.[39] The correspondent detailed how the person in question had resided in Grove Park, Rathmines, as well as a house in the nearby Stamer Street but had been ejected from both, going on to claim that the police were tracking this individual. It is perhaps important to clarify that Giri no longer lived at Grove Park in this period, having moved to Lowell House, a premises on Herbert Avenue, a cul de sac off the Merrion Road between Sandymount and Booterstown on the south coast of the city. Whether or not any Indian students lived at No. 1 Grove Park by 1916 is unclear but at least one other Indian student lived in another property further along the street according to records for the academic year 1915–16 held in the King's Inns.[40] Presuming the letter to have been genuine, having denounced his classmate, the King's Inns student concluded with the feigned concern for not wishing to tar all students with the same brush reminiscent of previous comments in the *Eye-Opener*: 'I do not think that you should class all students as being bad – some are bad, most of them are good, and it is not good to blame the innocent for those who are guilty.'[41]

One could conclude the story of Indian students and the *Eye-Opener* at this point as an insight into the ugly side of xenophobia, gossip and libel which rarely features in the historical reconstitution of 1916 Dublin. However, it is worth following the subsequent fate of Thomas Dickson as it appears this attack on Indian students in the pages of the *Eye-Opener* likely played a decisive role in the editor's own demise.

On Easter Monday, 24 April, five days after the resolution of thanks was conveyed to the Lord Lieutenant, a rebellion broke out in Dublin. The details of this most pivotal event in modern Irish history will not be entered into here but one infamous saga of Easter 1916, the facts of which remain partially occluded to this day, will be examined.

On Wednesday morning, 26 April, while the insurrection was ongoing, Dickson was illegally executed in the aforementioned Portobello Barracks (now Cathal Brugha Barracks) in Rathmines. He was unlawfully executed without trial by firing squad alongside the outspoken radical activist Francis Sheehy-Skeffington and another newspaper editor, Patrick McIntyre. Their murder became an early *cause célèbre* in the wake of the Rising. The officer responsible for their killing, Captain J. C. Bowen Colthurst had, the night previously, shot dead an innocent teenager named James Coade. On

Wednesday 26 April, Bowen Colthurst also mortally wounded an unarmed captured rebel during a field interrogation.[42]

The broad facts of these events are well known and were the subject of a Royal Commission of Inquiry in August 1916. Around dusk on Tuesday 25 April, Sheehy-Skeffington had been detained by a military picket at Portobello Bridge and was conveyed under escort to Portobello barracks as a prisoner. He was subsequently removed from his cell and brought along as a 'hostage' – essentially a human shield – on a night-patrol which ultimately attacked the premises of Mr J. J. Kelly, a tobacconist and nationalist councillor on Dublin Corporation whose premises were located 200 metres on the other side of Portobello Bridge.[43]

After soldiers threw a bomb into Kelly's shop, four individuals were found inside. Two of these, Dickson and McIntyre, were arrested and brought to the barracks. The following morning, Sheehy-Skeffington, along with Dickson and McIntyre, was brought into a yard adjoining the barrack guard room and executed without trial by a firing squad under command of Captain Bowen Colthurst.

Neither in the published report of the Royal Commission or in subsequent accounts of this incident has the reason why Dickson and McIntyre were in Kelly's shop at the time of the raid been accounted for. Kelly himself was absent from his shop at the time of the raid. The Royal Commission recorded that 'Mr McIntyre, who was a friend of Alderman Kelly, had been on the premises some time and Mr Dickson, who lived close by, took refuge there when he heard the soldiers firing as they approached.'[44]

However, J. J. Kelly's sister, who was also in the shop during the raid, also gave evidence to the Royal Commission. Crucial parts of her testimony do not appear in the final report and are only preserved in press coverage of her statement. Miss Kelly recalled how 'McIntyre had come to see her brother about some Indian students. Dickson ran into the house when he heard the shooting by the military on the street.'[45]

The official version of this episode claims that it was pure chance that Dickson ended up in Kelly's shop on the night of 25 April. However, the Indian context makes this highly unlikely. One factor which makes this mystery difficult to solve is the fact that so little is known about Patrick McIntyre and the paper which he supposedly edited, *The Searchlight*. No paper bearing this title exists in the collections of the National Library of Ireland. It is known that McIntyre had previously been editor of an anti-Larkinite newspaper during the 1913 Dublin Lockout called *The Toiler*.[46]

The Toiler was rumoured to be funded by the industrialist William Martin Murphy.[47] It ceased publication at the end of 1914, suggesting that McIntyre may then have been seeking new employment.[48] In September 1914, a regular column began to appear in the *Meath Chronicle*. Entitled 'Searchlights', it was written under the pseudonym 'Tara' and resembled very much the content of the *Eye-Opener*, focussing on exposing scandals of both a moral and political character.[49] Tellingly, these 'Searchlights' no longer appeared after 22 April 1916, the same day that Dickson published his last paper before his death.[50] It seems credible, but by no means conclusive, that McIntyre could have been the author of these pieces. No anti-Indian content has been found among more than fifty editions of 'Searchlights' published in the *Meath Chronicle* leading to the possibility – and again this is by no means conclusive – that McIntyre was also in some way connected to Dickson's *Eye-Opener*.

Whether Miss Kelly confused Dickson and McIntyre or not, it would seem that it was true that Indian students were being discussed in Kelly's shop on the evening of 25 April as the rebellion intensified across the city of Dublin. The reason for Kelly's involvement in all of this appears to be much easier to establish. From its first issue right through to its last, one of the most consistent advertisers in Dickson's *Eye-Opener* was James J. Kelly, 35 and 36 Camden Street and 59 Dame Street. Among other advertising spaces not filled and 'reserved' for various businesses in the city, Kelly's back page advertisement encouraged readers to buy Juverna Cigarettes, 'Irish! Real Irish!'.[51] Piecing together all these details, it seems highly plausible that Miss Kelly's testimony was correct in stating that her brother had scheduled a meeting with McIntyre, Dickson, or both, on the evening or night of 25 April 1916 in order to discuss the articles relating to Indian students in the *Eye-Opener* and, perhaps, Kelly's continued commercial association with the paper.

In unravelling this episode, it is important to have established, after almost a century, the likely reason why Dickson and McIntyre were together in Kelly's shop when it was raided by British soldiers on 25 April. With relation to the Indian students, the murder of Dickson and McIntyre put an unexpected and abrupt end to the publication of the racist articles in the *Eye-Opener* at a time when police warnings had failed to change the paper's editorial policy on this matter.

Not only is this episode an important one in highlighting the fragility of that good will towards Indian students which is noted both in Giri's memoir and in the 1914 *National Student*, it also provides an important counterpoint to the assertion that Indian students in Dublin gravitated towards the advanced wings of Irish nationalism and republicanism and disavowed the Crown Government. In writing to the Lord Lieutenant, D. R. Kalia reflected positively upon the rule of Lord Hardinge in India, observing that establishing 'wholesome relations between the rulers and the ruled' had made the outgoing Viceroy a revered figure among the Indian people.[52] Yet again, enthusiasm for reform and evidence of loyalty among Indian students can be found here. This underlines the fact that these students were anything but monolithic in their views and opinions. In analysing an earlier phase of Indian encounter with British society, Antoinette Burton provides good justification for these divergences between Indian students. Of cultural identities, Burton points out that they are 'negotiable, contingent, and ever shifting, largely because they are the product not of inheritance or origins alone but of *politics* at the micro- and the macro levels, and in the most elastic sense of the word'.[53]

Police Searches and Giri's Last Days in Dublin

While the events of Easter 1916 put an abrupt and unforeseen end to the xenophobic campaign of the *Eye-Opener*, Indian students in Dublin faced new challenges in its aftermath. Again, conflicting attitudes of loyalty and disloyalty to the Crown and the British government in Ireland have been found among Dublin's Indian students. Regarding loyalty to the Crown, a large review of military and ambulance personnel who served during the Easter rebellion was held in the grounds of Trinity College Dublin on 13 May 1916. The *Irish Times* estimated that a thousand people were assembled on this parade which was reviewed by General Sir John Maxwell, then military governor of Ireland, and by the Prime Minister, Herbert Henry Asquith. The Prime Minister's arrival in Dublin the day before brought an abrupt end to the execution of rebel leaders which had been ongoing since 3 May.

Among the units and groups on this parade it is reported that 'Indian students of the King's Inns, who performed ambulance work, paraded with the Rathmines unit [of the Voluntary Aid Detachment]'.[54] This is the only reference which has been found to indicate that Indian students served in an ambulance and first-aid capacity during the 1916 Rising. While it gives tantalisingly little evidence about the nature of this service, it confirms conclusively that an unknown number of the Indian law students in Dublin were actively engaged in medical work during the hostilities. As already noted, at least one student at the King's Inns, though not one of the UCD contingent, Aftab Rai, served in the Indian Volunteer Ambulance Corps in Britain but this remains the only evidence found of any such unit on Irish soil. Questions such as whether this was an *ad hoc* formation or whether it was already established and parading prior to the outbreak of the insurrection remain, regrettably, unanswered.

In contrast to this image of imperial solidarity in the face of the freshly suppressed insurgency, Giri claims in his memoir to have developed friendships with members of the Irish Volunteers and the Irish Citizen Army (ICA), the two main armed bodies constituting the rebel forces. In particular, Giri notes that he became close to James Connolly, a leading figure in Irish and international socialism and leader of the Citizen Army. Of Connolly, Giri recollected:

> I remember vividly meeting Connolly on several occasions as I was regularly invited to their [Citizen Army] meetings … More than any of the leaders of the uprising it was Connolly who inspired me. I resolved that as soon as I returned to India I would give a graphic account of these struggles to inspire our own people. I also felt that, at the earliest opportunity, I would take up the organisation of the transport workers in the country so that, along with other nationalist forces, we would be in a position to jeopardise the movement of the troops. When a real conflict arose, the transport workers could become the bulwark of the national movement and thus subvert British authority.[55]

Although Giri's involvement in railway trade unionism dates back to 1922 when he became president of the Bengal Nagpur Railway Indian Labour Union – a springboard from which he succeeded in uniting the various railway unions of India into the All-India Railwaymen's Federation in 1923 –

Giri did not employ the tactic of an all-out railway strike until 1927. However, when the strike did occur, Giri managed to grow the resistance from a single station in Khargpur to a strike of an estimated 35,000 of the railway's 60,000 employees. This ground the Bengal–Nagpur line to a standstill for almost an entire month. Although the events of 1913–14 in Dublin differed from Giri's 1927 campaign in that the former was a lockout by employers and the latter was an actual strike, the results were the same: both unions represented some of the poorest workers and they were crippled into submission by employers who had deeper pockets, the support of police riot squads, and the luxury of time. In Dublin, those who came to prominence during the Lockout were blacklisted. In India, 2,000 workers from the workshop at Khargpur where the strike began were served with retrenchment notices in September 1928.[56] Events at Khargpur took a very Dublin twist thereafter when a fresh strike by workers was answered with a lockout by the railway company. However, unlike Dublin, the 90 day lockout ended successfully for the workers and Giri secured back-pay for the workers through skilful negotiating, playing Sir George Rainy of the Viceroy's executive council and the employers at the railway company into a compromise.[57]

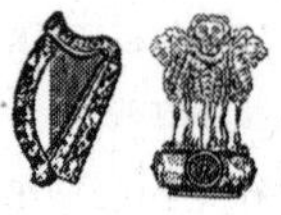

Chapter 9

Leaving Ireland

In the wake of the 1916 Rising, there was a heightened distrust in police and official circles about certain members of Dublin's Indian community. Giri recalls that there was 'a deep suspicion in the minds of the British Government in Ireland as well as at the India Office in London that I was not only connected with the Irish movement but that I was actively in league with it'.[1] Given that more people were arrested and deported after the 1916 Rising than actually took part in it, Indian students were no doubt under intense scrutiny at this time of frenetic activity by the military authorities.The army was now in control of various parts of Ireland where martial law had been declared. This even included districts that had played no active part in the rebellion. Suspicion over Giri led to raids on his lodgings but Giri states that nothing incriminating was found.[2] Despite this, Giri claims that the authorities were not satisfied; 'not convinced of my innocence … a notice was issued to me on 1 June 1916 directing me to leave U.K. by 1 July'.[3] Thus, Giri's time in Dublin came to an abrupt end.

Although no record of Giri's deportation order has been located either in the registered papers of the Irish Chief Secretary's Office, or in the records of the Indian Political Intelligence in the British Library in London, circumstantial evidence to substantiate the validity of his claim that he was ordered to leave Ireland after the Rising can be found. The case of another Indian student, T. A. Chettiar, closely echoes Giri's experience after the Rising.

Chettiar's case was brought up in the House of Commons after the Rising by the Irish Nationalist MP for South Donegal, John Gordon Swift MacNeill. As noted previously, Swift MacNeill was also Professor of Constitutional Law and the Law of Public and Private Wrongs at UCD where he became acquainted with many of Dublin's Indian students. On 1 June, Swift MacNeill put a question to Prime Minister Asquith inquiring:

> whether he is aware that two Dublin detective police officers visited on the 24th instant, Empire Day, the residence in Dublin of Mr. T. Adminaruyana Chettiar, a leading citizen of the Presidency of Madras, who has been living with his wife and son in Dublin for the purpose of qualifying for the Bar at the King's Inns, where he has passed most brilliant examinations, winning on several occasions the highest prizes, and that the police officers, having for several hours searched all Mr. Chettiar's papers, books, and effects, found nothing in the slightest degree which threw any suspicion on his loyalty and took nothing away from his house; whether he is aware that Mr. Chettiar, who has been subjected to this treatment, has for over twelve years rendered honorary service to the Government of India, having served as a special magistrate, vice-president of the local board, and honorary visitor of the Salem Gaol, has been exempted from the operations of the Arms Act in India, has been awarded in open Durbar the silver medal at the Coronation in 1911, which celebration, as well as that in 1903, he attended at Delhi, and has been asked to advise the Indian Government in several important matters,

> including Lord Morley's reform in the Indian Legislative Councils, and has organised nearly 100 co-operative societies in his native district; and whether, having regard to the indignity to which Mr. Chettiar has been subjected and the indignation and unrest which this incident has created among the Indian community, especially his fellow Indian students, and in Dublin and is likely to create in Berlin, he will take steps for an investigation of the circumstances and of the character of the information under which Mr. Chettiar's house was thus visited and searched by the police while his wife was ill, and for the vindication of Mr. Chettiar's character and an apology to him, and, through him, to the loyal subjects of our Indian Empire who are aggrieved at this insult?[4]

The Prime Minister replied curtly that inquiries were being made into the matter. Swift MacNeill's parliamentary question sheds much light on the life of Chettiar. It has already been noted that, at thirty-seven years of age in 1916, Chettiar was much older than the majority of his classmates but his life experience as documented here shows that he was an individual of significant social standing prior to his arrival in Dublin. That the raid on Chettiar's house took place on Empire Day and that police appear certainly to have targeted the wrong man in this instance, suggests that something was suspected by authorities of the Indian students on this day. Empire Day was 24 May 1916, the birthday of the late Queen Victoria. Although celebrated since 1902, Empire Day was only officially recognised for the first time in 1916.[5] 24 May also happened to be the one month anniversary of the outbreak of the Easter rebellion. If Chettiar's was but one among several police raids to have occurred that day, the timeline fits in nicely with Giri's recollections. Although Giri misremembers the date upon which he was called to the Bar by almost a month – a date he gives only vaguely as 'the end of May', it is nonetheless plausible that the concrete dates he gives for his deportation order are accurate. It was on 1 June, while Swift MacNeill was interceding on Chettiar's behalf in the House of Commons, that Giri records he was issued with notice directing him to leave by 1 July.[6] Having successfully passed his final set of examinations at the King's Inns, Giri was called to the Bar on 21 June, again, a date that ties in well with the timeline presented in his autobiography and the context of the raid on Chettiar.[7]

Although successful in completing his qualification for the Bar, Giri was unable to finish his BA course at UCD. He reveals that it was his intention upon finishing his BA to travel onwards to Philadelphia to study for a Masters in Law and that he had also received offers of work in Dublin.[8] Rather than defining his exit from Dublin by the deportation order served upon him, Giri looked more positively upon his final weeks in Dublin. In concluding the chapter of his autobiography about his Irish days, Giri wrote:

> With the fervour inspired by the revolutionaries still fresh in my mind, I determined to return to India and take an active part in the political movement to secure the independence of my country.[9]

The fervour of which Giri wrote was not acquired merely by osmosis from having lived through the rebellion in Dublin city; Giri's own tutor, Thomas MacDonagh, had been among the first of the rebel leadership to have been executed on 3 May 1916. As already discussed, MacDonagh's revolutionary sentiments filtered into his teaching, something exemplified by Austin Clarke's recollection of MacDonagh dramatically producing a revolver during a lecture at UCD.

Whereas Giri left Ireland with a cloud of suspicion over his head and the echoes of insurrection ringing in his ears, the farewell afforded to departing Indian students a year later in the summer of 1917 was decidedly more convivial. On 13 June 1917, the Dublin Indian Association met at the Royal Hibernian Hotel on Dublin's Dawson Street to pay tribute to the recently qualified barristers preparing to set sail for India. As no records of this society have survived, it is unclear if this was the same society of which Giri was secretary for three years and which organised the 'South African Horrors' pamphlet which was shipped to India. In any case, at this much more salubrious and less radical affair in 1917, the Lord Chancellor and Chief Justice of Ireland presided and an opening address was delivered by Kanak Singh Roy, president of the association and son of Justice Harinath Roy of the Calcutta High Court.[10] A second gathering was held a fortnight later under the auspices of the Church of Ireland Young Men's Christian Association which expressed its friendship to the Indian Students' Association. There is a deeply loyalist and even subservient character attributed to the Indian students who spoke at this meeting in the *Irish Times*' report on it. It should be borne in mind that a strict culture of press censorship existed during the war and it is possible that the loyalty expressed was somewhat exaggerated either on the part of the speakers or the reporter present. In making his outgoing presidential address, the newly qualified Roy apparently spoke of the courtesy and manners which the Indian students had acquired in Ireland. 'It was not an inborn quality of the Indian; it had to be learned by experience. The Indian students had done their best to prove themselves worthy members of the community.'[11]Another student, S. N. Pal

> … said that the war had brought Indians and Britons together. Indians had come forward and shared the burden which Britain had to bear – the burden of the fight for democracy against autocracy … there now arose a common expectancy, a common loyalty. The Indians saw

> that it was now the business of the British Government to be in brotherhood with them, and not in rivalry.[12]

Nothing could contrast more sharply with the experience and sentiments of Giri as he departed.

Having learned under MacDonagh and having come into contact with Connolly and other radicals, Giri had received a baptism in revolution similar to that which created committed revolutionists across Ireland at this time. While the new political movement in Ireland never abated after the Rising, when Giri returned to India, he was transported from the chaos of Dublin to relative normality. Giri immediately became a member of the Indian National Congress and attended the Lucknow Congress in 1916. However, for five years he lived a relatively normal existence, practicing law with his father in Berhampur.[13] It was only following his reconnection with Gandhi that Giri's political involvement intensified. Giri withdrew from legal practice in order to comply with the principle of non-cooperation. He joined the *satyagraha* campaign at its inception in 1921. By February 1922, Giri found himself in prison for picketing shops selling alcohol. There, he led a successful hunger-strike and, upon his release, led a strike of transport workers. Giri's work with the All-India Railwaymen's Federation is something which one of his biographers has rightly picked up upon as bearing close resemblance to the situation which greeted Giri on his arrival in Dublin during the 1913 Lockout when James Larkin used the Irish Transport and General Workers' Union to take on the Dublin employers.[14]

Giri was by no means the only one of the Dublin law students to involve himself in politics upon his return to India. Gurdal Singh Salariya entered the King's Inns at Michaelmas 1915 and attended UCD for the year beginning autumn 1916. He was called to the Irish Bar on 5 June 1918 alongside fourteen other Indian students, five Irish students and a student born in Accra in the Gold Coast Colony (modern-day Ghana). In November 1916, Salariya was among a group who established a social club for Indian residents in Dublin.[15] Very little is known about this club except for the fact that it was established with the aim of providing a space for 'indoor games, a library, and the facilities for socials' for Indians in the city.[16] By 1919, Salariya was back in his native Amritsar at a time when Punjab was descending into violence.

Just as Ireland and Britain were subjected to Defence of the Realm legislation during the First World War, India had been placed under the Defence of India Act in 1915. In 1919, a subsequent act was passed to make aspects of these measures permanent so as to combat the Indian independence movement. Known as the Rowlatt Act after its author, Sir Sidney Arthur Taylor Rowlatt, the legislation caused Gandhi to call for mass non-violent civil-disobedience through the principle of *satyagraha*. In Amritsar, two leaders of the Indian independence movement were secretly deported from the district in early April. Protests erupted as news of this spread. On 10 April, soldiers opened fire on a gathering at a railway bridge in Amritsar. Four were killed. Salariya was among the crowd and, as the crowd began to retaliate, Salariya and another lawyer, Maqbool Mahmood, appealed for calm on both sides. Salariya and Mahmood's appeal was futile and the soldiers responded to a volley of stones with rifle fire, killing approximately twenty further demonstrators.[17]

Mahmood recorded his experience of the incident to the Indian National Congress as follows:

> Salaria [sic] and I shouted out to the Deputy Commissioner [R. B. Beckett] and the officers to get back and not to fire, as we still hoped to take the crowd back. A few of the crowd threw wood and stones at the soldiers. The soldiers at once opened a volley of fire without any warning or

> intimation. Bullets whistled to my right and left. The crowd dispersed, leaving 20 or 25 killed and wounded. After the firing stopped, I went up to the soldiers and enquired if they had an ambulance car or any first aid arrangements at hand, I wanted to run to the hospital which was close by for help. The soldiers would not allow me…The Deputy Commissioner himself was present when the fire was opened. He knew that Salaria and I were members of the Bar, and were trying to get the people back to the city. It was by mere accident that our lives were saved.[18]

These killings at the railway bridge was a key event in the prelude to a much larger and infamous massacre which occurred at Jallianwalla Bagh, a walled garden near the sacred Sikh Golden Temple in Amritsar three days later on Sunday, 13 April 1919. There, troops under the command of General Reginald Dyer subjected a trapped crowd to ten minutes of sustained gunfire. Dyer recorded 1,650 rounds as having been expended by his troops over the course of ten minutes. The death toll at Jallianwala Bagh remains a point of contention. The Indian National Congress commission put the death toll at 1,200 with 3,600 wounded. The official figure given by the government was 379 dead and approximately three times that number wounded. In a final Irish link to the events of 1919 in Amritsar, the lieutenant-governor of the Punjab at the time was an Irishman, Michael O'Dwyer. He had ordered the deportations which sparked the violence on 10 April that led to the massacre at Jallianwalla Bagh. O'Dwyer defended Dyer's actions strenuously. On 13 March 1940, echoing what had happened to William Hutt Curzon Wyllie in 1909, an Indian nationalist shot and killed O'Dwyer at a lecture hosted by the Royal Central Asian Society and the East India Association in Caxton Hall in London.

Turning back to India, the JallianwallaBagh became a mobilising event in the Indian independence struggle. As events gathered pace in 1920 and 1921, yet another one of Dublin's law students came to prominence. The aforementioned Polisetty Hanumayya Gupta, who joined both the King's Inns and UCD simultaneous to Giri, became a leading member of the independence movement in Guntur district. He was instrumental to coordinating hartal (a general strike extending to all aspects of the community) in July 1921 in reaction to the imprisonment of nationalists including his fellow Dublin law student, the aforementioned Shri Unnava Lakshminarayana.[19] Gupta was arrested for his role in this on 29 July 1921. Lakshminarayana and Gupta appear to have been close to one and other. Earlier, in January 1920, the two Dublin-educated lawyers were among those who resolved to suspend practice of the law following the resolution of the Calcutta Special Congress of the Indian National Congress.[20]

By December of 1921, Gupta had been released and was involved in a taxation boycott. By then he was a member of the Andhra Provincial Congress Committee and was corresponding directly with Gandhi to coordinate the boycott.[21] In a tactic that echoed the situation he found in Dublin, Gupta formed a volunteer force in Guntur at this time. Unlike the Irish Volunteers in Dublin, Gupta's volunteers were unarmed and their role was to encourage (or enforce) compliance with the hartal ongoing in the district.

Having given some insight into Dublin Indian students' subsequent participation in the 1919–21 phase of the Indian independence struggle, it is appropriate to return to Giri. It is unnecessary here to go into a detailed history of Giri's subsequent involvement in the Indian independence struggle, this has been covered in detail by his biographers. To skip forward to the period after Indian independence was achieved in 1947, Giri was appointed High Commissioner in Ceylon (modern-day Sri-Lanka). In 1952, he was elected to India's lower house of parliament, the Lok Sabha, where he took up the portfolio of Minister for Labour. Giri resigned from government in 1954 when his cabinet colleagues sided against him in an industrial dispute. Giri served as governor of various provinces for ten years beginning in 1957. Around this time he wrote two major works: *Industrial Relations* (1955) and *Labour Problems in India* (1959). Giri became Vice President of India in 1967 before succeeding to the Presidency of India in August 1969.[22]

Conclusion

In examining the lives and experiences of Indian law students in Dublin between 1913 and 1916, much new light has been shed on the nature of contact between natives and visitors to the city in these years of turbulence and transformation. On an official level, both in their dealings with the institutions in which they studied and with the state in the form of police and officers of the India Office, their experience underlined the inequality of Indians among British and Irish subjects. Among their classmates and teachers, their encounters appear to have been decisively more positive. The intercession by Professor Swift MacNeill on behalf of T. A. Chettiar in the aftermath of the 1916 Rising exemplifies the tenacious assertion of equality by certain Irish nationalists of their Indian friends. Similarly, the affectionate if irreverent memorialisation of Indian students by their classmates in the *National Student* is evidence of their integration into the social life of the university.

Outside student circles, or perhaps through them, Indian students linked in to advanced Irish nationalist networks. Through the anonymously published articles by Indians in the *Irish Volunteer* and the *National Student*, it is clear that Irish nationalists saw in these contributors allies in anti-imperialism and valued their ability to highlight the failures of British governance beyond the shores of Ireland. It is important to stress that Dublin's Indian students were not a monolith and in their published contributions, the themes of reform and anti-imperialism come through at different points.

It is also important to consider the ways in which Indian–Irish associations fostered in this period bore fruit in later years. In 1920, Éamon de Valera, then President of the provisional government of the Irish Republic, published a pamphlet entitled *India and Ireland*, the text of an address he had given in New York to the Friends of Freedom for India on 28 February 1920 while on a fundraising mission to the United States. Paraphrasing George Washington, de Valera asserted 'Patriots of India, your cause is identical with ours.'[1]

While in San Francisco in July 1919, de Valera was presented with a sword and flag by Gopal Singh and Jagat Singh, representatives of the radical militant Ghadar party.[2] In 1964, a predecessor of Giri's in the presidency, Sarvepalli Radhakrishnan visited Ireland. De Valera, then President of Ireland, took great pleasure in producing the sword he had been given by the Ghadars back in 1919 and showing it to his Indian counterpart.[3]

As President of India after 1969, Giri frequently expressed his intention to travel to Ireland, an ambition that was diligently charted by the Irish Embassy in Delhi throughout Giri's presidency. In 1972, Iremonger reported that '[Giri] "does not care" when he goes [to Europe] "so long as he gets to Ireland"'.[4] Giri had also received an invitation from British Prime Minister Ted Heath around this time and the Irish Ambassador reported back to Dublin with amusement that 'in respond[ing] to Mr. Heath's invitation to visit England he [Giri] said that he would "drop into" London on his way to Ireland'.[5] Giri clearly developed a good rapport with Iremonger during the latter's term as ambassador.[6] Once, at a tea party for the heads of diplomatic missions in Delhi, Giri spent up to fifteen minutes with Iremonger. The ambassador noted 'This was rather a long time to be with the President at such a function' – and the President spent much time reminiscing on his days in Ireland. In his conversations with Iremonger, Giri remembered his former tutor, Thomas MacDonagh, and reiterated a sentiment which he had expressed to Irish officials in India previously that 'when I am not an Indian I am an Irishman'.[7]

Arrangements for Giri's arrival were at an advanced stage early in 1974 as it seemed quite certain that the President would travel to Europe to visit Belgium and Ireland.[8] Ultimately, Giri was unable to fulfil his wish to travel to Ireland owing to a combination of unavoidable commitments in India and concerns over his health. On this last point, it should be noted that, approaching his eightieth birthday – and contemplating re-election – in 1974, the President remained 'remarkably active for his age'.[9] One of Giri's strongest reasons for wishing to travel to Ireland was to meet de Valera, of whom he had spoken so warmly in his memoir and who represented one of the sole surviving Irish nationalists with whom Giri would have been acquainted during his time as a student in Dublin.[10] In August 1974, Giri's term as president of India concluded. A year later, at the age of ninety-two, Éamon de Valera died, thus bringing the possibility of this encounter to an end.

During the early 1970s, a certain amount of lore and exaggeration was generated about the nature and extent of Giri's earlier connections with Ireland. While these are not helpful to the historian trying to separate fact from invention in rebuilding a picture of early twentieth-century Dublin, the reconnection between Giri and Ireland should be viewed as a distinct chapter in its own right in the context of a long history of revolutionary associations between two nations which share a remarkable degree of common experience despite their geographical distance. As the elder statesmen, and the custodians of real connections dating back to pre-independence, the past held a special contemporary significance both for Giri and de Valera.

Returning to Giri's student days, the present focus on commemorations provides an opportunity not to re-enshrine the story of Ireland's revolutionary decade as was done in the 1960s and 1970s. Rather it calls upon historians to reinvestigate the forgotten and overlooked aspects of the period. In re-incorporating the history of Dublin's Indian student population into the social fabric of Dublin in these years it is hoped this short work sheds some new light on Dublin of a century ago. It has been shown that the Indian students were not merely witness to the formative events of these years. They were intimately associated with the Irish radical élite. When rebellion broke out, they were swept up in the conflict like so many of Dublin's citizenry. Whether tending to the wounded as ambulance volunteers during the Rising or living in fear of raids and deportation in its wake, the events of Easter 1916 profoundly impacted upon these students. However, the seismic events of Easter should not eclipse all that preceded it. From 1913 onwards, in writing for radical and student publications, in meeting advanced nationalists, feminists and socialists, and in immersing themselves in a city that awaited the establishment of the first domestic parliament in over a century, the politics of India and Ireland intersected among Dublin's Indian law students. It has been possible to show how the politics of Ireland had an effect on the Indians living here. What remains, if it is even possible, is for historians to trace the impact these students had on Irish ideas and attitudes at the dawn of an era when empire began to crumble on Britain's east and its west.

Endnotes

Acknowledgements

1 V. V. Giri, *My Life and Times, Volume I* (Delhi, 1976), p. 14.

2 Ibid., p.33.

Introduction

1 Valentine Iremonger to R. McDonagh, 17 November 1972 (NAI DFA 2001/27/198).

2 Goetz Nordbruch, 'Arab Students in Weimar Germany – Politics and Thought Beyond Borders', *Journal of Contemporary History*, xlix, no. 2 (April 2014), pp 275–295 and Thomas Weber, *Our Friend 'The Enemy': Elite Education in Britain and Germany before World War I* (Stanford, 2008).

3 Liping Bu, 'The Challenge of Race Relations: American Ecumenism and Foreign Student Nationalism, 1900–1940', *Journal of American Studies*, xxxv, no. 2 (August, 2001), pp 217–237; Barbara M. Posadas and Roland L. Guyotte, 'Unintentional Immigrants: Chicago's Filipino Foreign Students Become Settlers, 1900–1941', *Journal of American Ethnic History*, ix, no. 2 (Spring, 1990), pp 26–48; Julie Hessler, 'Death of an African Student in

Moscow: Race, Politics, and the Cold War', *Cahiers du Monde Russe*, xlvii, no. 1/2, (January – June, 2006), pp 33–63; and Martha Hanna, 'French Women and American Men: "Foreign" Students at the University of Paris, 1915–1925', *French Historical Studies*, xxii, no. 1 (Winter, 1999), pp 87–112.

4 Antoinette Burton, *At the Heart of the Empire: Indians and the Colonial Encounter in Late-Victorian Britain* (Berkeley, 1998), p. 26.

5 Burton, *At the Heart of the Empire*, p. 27.

6 On Noyk's nationalist and republican links see Michael Noyk's witness statement to the Bureau of Military History, 4 July 1952 (Military Archives of Ireland, BMH, WS 707).

7 On the somewhat convoluted lineage of the various educational institutions which occupied premises on St Stephen's Green between 1854 and 1909 see Donal McCartney, *UCD, a National Idea: The History of University College Dublin* (Dublin, 1999), pp 1–24.

8 Kettle was only an MP between 1906 and 1910, having lost his Tyrone East seat in the December 1910 general election. Swift MacNeill was MP for South Donegal (1887–1918). See Brian M. Walker, *Parliamentary Election Results in Ireland, 1801–1922* (Dublin, 1978).

9 See Minutes of 23 May 1916, *University College Dublin Governing Body Minute Book* 4, 23 March 1915 to 20 March 1917 (IE, UCDA, GV2/4).

10 Minutes of 11 May 1915, *University College Dublin Governing Body Minute Book 4, 23 March 1915 to 20 March 1917* (IE UCDA, GV2/4).

11 Women were only freed of this restriction in 1919 with the Sex Disqualification (Removal) Act (1919), the year after women over thirty had been granted the right to vote. The first woman to be called to the Irish Bar was Frances Christian Kyle in November 1921. Kenneth Fergusson

(ed.), *King's Inns Barristers, 1868–2004* (Dublin, 2005), p. 27.

12 Fergusson, *King's Inns Barristers* and *University College Dublin Calendar for the Session 1914–15* (Dublin, 1914), pp 324–5.

13 Ibid., p. 1.

14 Ibid., p. 21.

15 Ibid., p. 27.

16 Minutes signed 1 November 1913, Benchers' Minute Book, 1901-17, pp 353–4 (Library of the Honourable Society of King's Inns, Dublin).

Chapter 1 – Irish and Imperial Contexts

1 Rozina Visram, *Ayahs, Lascars, and Princes: Indians in Britain: 1700–1947* (London, 1986) pp 77–8.

2 See Visram, *Ayahs, Lascars, and Princes*, p. 78.

3 Alex Tickell, 'Scholarship-terrorists: the India House Hostel and the "student problem" in Edwardian London' in Rehana Ahmed and Sumita Mukherjee (eds), *South Asian Resistances in Britain, 1858–1947* (London, 2011) p. 9.

4 Shompa Lahiri, *Indians in Britain: Anglo-Indian Encounters, Race, and Identity, 1880–1930* (London, 2000), p. 7.

5 See Lahiri, *Indians in Britain*, p. 7.

6 Antoinette Burton, *At the Heart of the Empire: Indians and the Colonial Encounter in Late-Victorian Britain* (Berkeley, 1998), p. 26.

7 See Lahiri, *Indians in Britain* p. 5.

8 See Burton, *At the Heart of the Empire*, p. 26.

9 *East India (Indian Students' Department). Report on the Work of the Indian Students' Department*, July 1913–June 1914, 1 [Cd 7719], H.C. 1914-16, xlviii, p. 3.

10 V. V. Giri, *My Life and Times, Volume I* (Delhi, 1976), p. 14.

16. Jennie Wyse Power, prominent nationalist and feminist. She later established a vegetarian restaurant at 21 Henry Street which served as a meeting place for radicals in Dublin. It was there that the 1916 proclamation was signed prior to the Rising. This photograph of Wyse Power was taken during her time as an agrarian activist with the Ladies' Land League (courtesy of Kilmainham Gaol Archives).

17. An advert for Jennie Wyse Power's Irish Farm Produce Café, which appeared in *An Claidheamh Soluis*. Directly above is an advert for Tom Clarke's tobacconists and newsagents. Clarke was at the very centre of the planning of the 1916 Rising (courtesy of UCD National Folklore Collection).

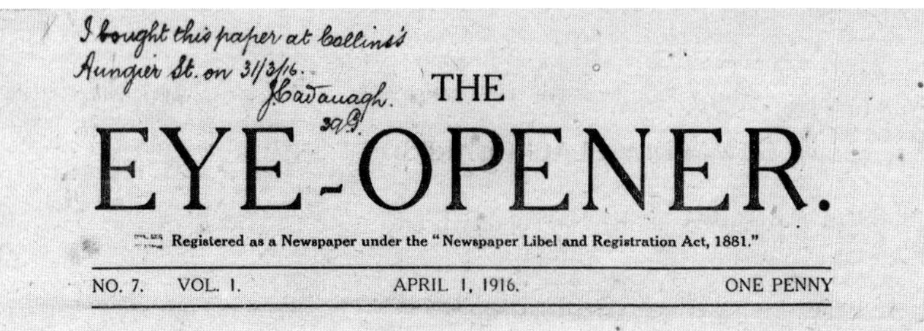
I bought this paper at Collins's Aungier St. on 31/3/16. J Cavanagh.

THE

EYE-OPENER.

Registered as a Newspaper under the "Newspaper Libel and Registration Act, 1881."

NO. 7. VOL. I. APRIL 1, 1916. ONE PENNY

18. Masthead of the *Eye-Opener*, 1 April 1916. A manuscript note in the top left hand corner is from a detective of the Dublin Metropolitan Police who bought this copy on Aungier Street and put it on file whilst investigating the paper (NAI CSORP 1916/9070. Courtesy of the National Archives of Ireland).

Irish ! Real Irish !

JUVERNA
CIGARETTES

10 for 4d.

JAMES J. KELLY,
35 and 36 Camden Street, and
59 Dame Street, DUBLIN.

Ask your Tobacconist for them.

19. An advertisement for James J. Kelly's shop, which appeared regularly in the *Eye-Opener* (NAI CSORP 1916/9070. Courtesy of the National Archives of Ireland).

CSO/RP/1916/9070

"Copy of the Resolution"

"We the Indian students resident in Dublin, assembled in this public meeting, held at the College Hotel on the 17th of April 1916, beg to place on record our heartfelt gratitude to H. E. the Lord Lieutenant of Ireland for his so kindly expressing his sympathy with the Indian students and for the action he has so graciously taken in warning the owners, publishers & printers of the Eye-Opener and thus protecting the Indians from the scurrilous attacks."

Proposed by Mr B. N. Agasti
Seconded by Mr J. N. Ma[illegible]

CHIEF SECRETARY'S
9070 – 20 MAY 1916
OFFICE

19. April 16

Dear Sir, 2580

I have the honour to forward herewith a copy of the resolution passed in a public meeting of the Indian Students, with the request that you will very kindly lay it before H. E. the Lord Lieutenant.

Thanking you in anticipation
I am
Yours truly
Abdur Razzaq.
President of the meeting

Received from P.S. Vice Regal Lodge
Put with papers
[illegible]
21/4

20. A copy of the resolution of gratitude sent by Indian students to Viscount Wimborne, the Lord Lieutenant of Ireland, 19 April 1916 thanking him for his actions in relation to the *Eye-Opener* newspaper (NAI CSORP 1916/9070. Courtesy of the National Archives of Ireland).

21. 'Kelly's Corner', the premises of J. J. Kelly, tobacconist and cigar bonder, on the corner of Camden Street and Harcourt Street, Dublin. It was there that Thomas Dickson and Patrick McIntyre were taken prisoner during the 1916 Rising. Along with Francis Sheehy Skeffington, they were executed without trial by Captain J. C. Bowen-Colthurst the following morning (photograph by author).

22. A view of the destruction Dublin. Nelson's Pillar, as seen fr Henry Street through the rub of the GPO, in the aftermath of t Easter Rising (Desmond FitzGer Photographs, IE UCDA P80/PH digital image (c) UCD Digital Libr http://dx.doi.org/10.7925/dr ucdlib_30686, reproduced by ki permission of UCD Archives).

23. Éamon de Valera, future President of the Executive Council, Taoiseach, and President of Ireland. De Valera was commandant of the 3rd (Dublin) Battalion of the Irish Volunteers during the 1916 Rising. Pictured here under arrest following the insurrection (papers of Éamon de Valera, IE UCDA P150/523, reproduced by kind permission of the UCD-OFM Partnership).

24. T. Adinavayana Chettiar, law student at UCD and the King's Inns. Chettiar topped his law class in 1915 and was awarded that year's Dunbar Barton prize. He was called to the Irish Bar in Hilary term 1917 (courtesy of Österreichische National-bibliothek (National Library of Austria), Esperanto collection, inventory no. 701482.C.19.6).

J. G. Swift MacNeill "on the war path."

Cartoon by "Spy." By courtesy of the Proprietors of "Vanity Fair." 15

25. A caricature of J.G. Swift MacNeill, MP for South Donegal (1887-1918), Professor of Constitutional Law and the Law of Public and Private Wrongs at UCD. Swift MacNeill defended Chettiar at Westminster following a police raid on Chettiar's residence on 24 May 1916 (caricature by 'Spy', *Vanity Fair*, 13 March 1902).

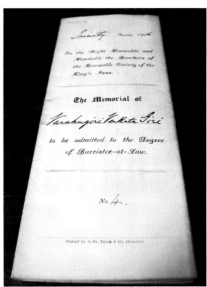

26. Report showing V.V. Giri's final examination results from King's Inns, June 1916 (courtesy of the Library of the Honourable Society of King's Inns).

27. V. V. Giri's Bar Certificate, which he was awarded from King's Inns on 21 June 1916 (courtesy of the Library of the Honourable Society of King's Inns).

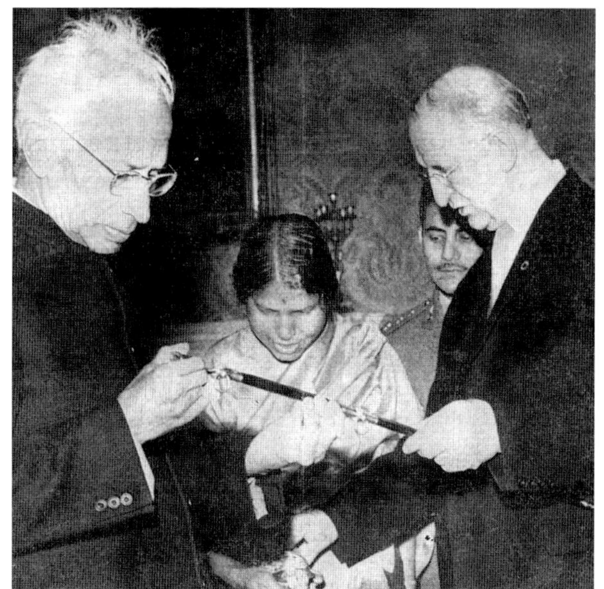

28. President of Ireland, Éamon de Valera, displays the sword he received from an Indian delegation in San Francisco in 1919 to the Indian President Sarvepalli Radhakrishnan and Indian Deputy Minister of External Affairs Lakshmi N. Menon during the state visit of 1964 (*Evening Press*, 22 September 1964, National Archives of Ireland, PRES/1/P6020/1. Courtesy of the National Archives of Ireland).

University honours India's President

AN honorary degree of Doctor of Law was conferred on President Radhakrishnan of India by the President, Mr. de Valera, Chancellor of the National University, in Iveagh House, Dublin, yesterday evening.

Irish impact on thought

THINGS THAT BIND INDIA TO IRELAND

LAYS WREATH TO 1916 PATRIOTS

Talks held on turf dispute

Anniversary of company celebrated

Horse Show team for Wembley

Cattle cards 'tampered with'

£860,000 coiners' hoard seized

WALKOUT AT STRASBOURG

29. President Sarvepalli Radhakrishnan, pictured with President of Ireland, Éamon de Valera (right of picture), and Michael Tierney, President of UCD (far left of picture), receiving an honorary law degree from UCD (*Irish Press*, 23 September 1964, reproduced courtesy of the National Library of Ireland).

DFA/2001/27/365

CONFIDENTIAL
P.R. 6/72

28 January 1972

Hugh McCann, Esq.,
Secretary
Department of Foreign Affairs
Dublin

<u>President Giri & Ireland</u>

Dear Secretary,

Please refer to our previous correspondence regarding a possible visit by President Giri to Ireland.

On the 25 January when he granted an audience to Mr. & Mrs. Kenny he again spoke about his experiences in Ireland and of his determination to visit Ireland as soon as he could find it possible. During the course of our conversation he mentioned once again that his tutor at University College Dublin had been Thomas McDonagh (executed in 1916). He also mentioned that because of his expulsion from Ireland by the British in 1916 he was unable to take his final exams at UCD but that by then he had taken his final law examinations and had been admitted as a Barrister at Kings Inns, Dublin. He said rather vehemently in regard to his travelling that he "does not care" when he goes "so long as he gets to Ireland". You will recall that in my previous reports I mentioned that in respond to Mr. Heath's invitation to visit England he said that he would "drop into" London on his way to Ireland.

Previously at the tea party held for the Heads of Diplomatic Missions in Delhi on the 23 January the President had called me over and spoke at some length (upto 15 minutes) about Ireland and his recollections of his long stay there. This was rather a long time to be with the President at such a function but once again he said - as he said to Mr. Kenny - "when I am not an India I am an Irishman".

It is clearly his intention to visit Ireland as soon as he can fit it into his programme. In connection with his revelation that due to his expulsion from Ireland he was unable to takehis final exams at UCD the question of the confering on him of an Honorary Degree by the NUI might be raised when the time comes.

I still am of the opinion that his visit would have to be an official one and that a stay of mere two days would not be enough to satisfy him. My feeling is that he would expect to stay in Ireland from anything upto a week.

Yours sincerely,

30. A confidential 1972 report from the Irish Embassy in Delhi regarding President Giri and his connections with Ireland (Embassy of Ireland, Delhi, Confidential Report P. R. 6/72, 'President Giri & Ireland', 28 Jan. 1972, National Archives of Ireland, DFA 2001/27/365. Courtesy of the National Archives of Ireland).

11 *East India (Indian Students' Department). Report on the work of the Indian Students' Department, July 1913–June 1914*, 1 [Cd 7719], H.C. 1914–16, xlviii, p. 3.
12 *East India (Indian Students' Department). Report on the work of the Indian Students' Department,* July 1913–June 1914, 2 [Cd 7719], H.C. 1914–16, xlviii, p. 4.
13 Ibid.
14 See Tickell, 'Scholarship-terrorists', p.14.
15 On the Lee Warner Committee, see Tickell, 'Scholarship-terrorists', p. 10 *et seq.*
16 See Tickell, 'Scholarship-terrorists', p. 11.
17 See Lahiri, *Indians in Britain*, p. 15.
18 *Irish Times*, 17 April 1914.
19 Ibid.
20 See Tickell, 'Scholarship-terrorists', p. 9.

Chapter 2 – Changing Attitudes to Indians in Britain, 1907–13

1 F. H. Brown, 'Warner, Sir William Lee- (1846–1914)', rev. Katherine Prior, *Oxford Dictionary of National Biography*, Oxford University Press, 2004; online edition, January 2012. [http://www.oxforddnb.com/view/article/34472, accessed 5 October 2015].
2 For an oral memoir of *Bean na hÉireann* and Inghinidhe na hÉireann, see interview with Sydney Gifford Czira, broadcast on 19 May 1971 and available via RTÉ Archives [http://www.rte.ie/archives/2014/0402/606021-cumann-na-mban-and-anti-women-irb/; accessed 12 November 2015].
3 *Bean na hÉireann*, July 1909, issue 10, p. 8.
4 *Bean na hÉireann*, August 1909, issue 11, pp 8–9.
5 Ibid.
6 Ibid.
7 *Bean na hÉireann*, September 1909, issue 12, p. 8.

8 Helena Molony, BMH WS 391, pp 18–19.
9 Patrick Sarsfield O'Hegarty, BMH WS 839, p. 5.
10 Patrick Sarsfield O'Hegarty, BMH WS 839, pp 7–8.
11 W. B. Yeats, 'Introduction' in Rabindranath Tagore, *Gitanjali (Song Offerings): a Collection of Prose Translations made by the Author from the Original Bengali* (London, 1912), p. x.
12 Malcolm Sen, 'Mythologising a "Mystic": W. B. Yeats on the poetry of Rabindranath Tagore', *History Ireland*, xviii, no. 4, [special issue: 'The Elephant and Partition: Ireland and India'] (July/August 2010), p. 21.
13 Irish Government News Service [press release], 'Minister Flanagan welcomes gift of WB Yeats bust to be presented to India', 10 September 2014 [http://www.merrionstreet.ie/en/News-Room/Releases/minister-flanagan-welcomes-gift-of-wb-yeats-bust-to-be-presented-to-india.html; accessed 6 November 2015].

Chapter 3 – Indian Law Students Arrive in Ireland

1 1911 census [see www.census.nationalarchives.ie; accessed 12 November 2015].
2 Rozina Visram, *Ayahs, Lascars, and Princes: Indians in Britain: 1700–1947* (London, 1986) pp 9 and 18.
3 See Visram, *Ayahs, Lascars, and Princes.*
4 Michael Kennedy, '"Where's the Taj Mahal?": Indian restaurants in Dublin since 1908', *History Ireland*, xviii, no. 4, [special issue: 'The Elephant and Partition: Ireland and India'] (July/August 2010), p. 50.
5 Adil Hussain Khan, 'Muslim students in 1950s Dublin', *History Ireland*, xviii, no. 4, [special issue: 'The Elephant and Partition: Ireland and India'] (July/August 2010), pp 44–5.
6 Central Statistics Office, *Census 2011 Profile 6: Migration and Diversity – A Profile of Diversity in Ireland* (Dublin, 2012),

p. 7 [http://www.cso.ie/en/media/csoie/census/documents/census2011profile6/Profile,6,Migration,and,Diversity,entire,doc.pdf; accessed 5 November 2015]. The number of Indians living in Ireland in 2002 was 2,534, meaning there was a 570 per cent increase in numbers in the ten years from 2002 to 2011.

7 The S. S. Simla was launched 13 October 1894, sunk by U-39 45 miles NWxW of Gozo, Malta, 2 April 1916, [see http://www.clydesite.co.uk/clydebuilt/viewship.asp?id=15018; accessed 23 October 2015].

8 V. V. Giri, *My Life and Times, Volume I* (Delhi, 1976), p. 13.

9 Antoinette Burton, *At the Heart of the Empire: Indians and the Colonial Encounter in Late-Victorian Britain* (Berkeley, 1998), pp 175–6.

10 See Giri, *Life and Times*, p. 13.

11 Ibid.

12 Ibid., p. 14.

13 Ibid., p. 12.

14 G. S. Bhargava, *V. V. Giri: Portrait of a President* (Delhi, 1970), pp 27–8.

15 Trinity College Dublin, Entrance books, 1896-1915 (Department of Manuscripts, Trinity College Dublin, TCD MUN/V/24).

16 Fergusson, *King's Inns Barristers*, pp. 211 and 311.

17 *Dublin University Calendar for the year 1912–13, Vol. II* (Dublin, 1913), p. 82.

18 Ibid., pp 94 and 96.

19 Trinity College Dublin, Entrance books, 1896–1915 (Department of Manuscripts, Trinity College Dublin, TCD MUN/V/24).

20 *UCD Calendar for the Session 1914–15* (Dublin, 1914) and Fergusson, *King's Inns Barristers*.

21 *UCD Calendar for the Session 1914–15* (Dublin, 1914); *UCD Calendar for the Session 1915–16* (Dublin, 1915); *UCD*

Calendar for the Session 1916–17 (Dublin, 1916); and *UCD Calendar for the Session 1917–18* (Dublin, 1917).

22 *Freeman's Journal*, 22 October 1915.

23 Data derived from Fergusson, *King's Inns Barristers.*

24 *Hansard 5 (Commons)*, lxxxii, col. 2922.

25 T. Adinarayana Chettiar, 'Esperants [sic] – What can it do for India', *East and West* (September 1905), iv, no. 47. Cited in *Luzac's Oriental List Volume XVI, January to December 1905* (Chicago, 1905), p. 224.

26 G. Satyamurty, 'Father of the co-operative movement', *The Hindu*, 6 January 2009.

Chapter 4 – Studying in a City in Turmoil: Lockout, War and Revolution

1 Michael Laffan, 'The emergence of the "Two Irelands", 1912–25', *History Ireland*, xii, no. 4 (Winter 2004) pp 40–44.

2 *Irish Volunteer*, 7 March 1914.

3 P. S. T. Sayee [Pangulury Sesha Thalpasaye] to Éamon de Valera, 12 June 1948 (Frank Aiken Papers, IE UCDA, P104/4806), quoted in Kate O'Malley, *Ireland, India and Empire: Indo-Irish Radical Connections, 1919–64* (Manchester, 2008), p. 167.

4 I am grateful to Kate O'Malley for her very generous assistance in trying to ascertain Sayee's connections with the Irish Volunteers.

5 Seamus Ua Caomhánaigh, BMH WS 889, p. 134.

6 On Gupta in India, see B. Seshagiri Rao, *History of Freedom Movement in Guntur District, 1921-1947* (Ongole, n.d.), p.127 and I am grateful to Spurti Subramanyam for bringing this source to my attention.

7 *Irish Volunteer*, 7 March 1914.

8 Ibid.

9 *Irish Volunteer*, 7 March 1914.

10 E. W. Ives, 'Henry VIII (1491–1547)', *Oxford Dictionary of National Biography* (Oxford, 2004: online edition, January 2008) [http://www.oxforddnb.com/view/article/12955; accessed 29 October 2015].
11 *Irish Volunteer*, 7 March 1914.
12 Ibid.

Chapter 5 – Subversion and Student Societies

1 V. V. Giri, *My Life and Times, Volume I* (Delhi, 1976), p. 33.
2 Minutes of 25 October 1916, Benchers' Minute Book, 1901–17(Library of the Honourable Society of King's Inns, Dublin), p. 445.
3 Record book of the Law Students' Debating Society (Library of the Honourable Society of King's Inns, Dublin), p. 57.
4 All information from Julitta Clancy (comp.) and Margaret Connolly (ast.), 'Alphabetical' index to Barristers' memorials, 1868–1968 in Kenneth Fergusson (ed.), *King's Inns Barristers, 1868–2004* (Dublin, 2005).
5 Record book of the Law Students' Debating Society (Library of the Honourable Society of King's Inns, Dublin), p. 65.
6 Benchers' Minute Book, 1901–17 (Library of the Honourable Society of King's Inns, Dublin) , p. 348.
7 Minutes of 12 January 1914, Benchers' Minute Book, 1901–17, p. 361 (Library of the Honourable Society of King's Inns, Dublin).
8 Minutes of 26 October 1914, Benchers' Minute Book, 1901–17, p. 382 (Library of the Honourable Society of King's Inns, Dublin).
9 Minutes of 14 April 1915, Benchers' Minute Book, 1901–17, p. 395 (Library of the Honourable Society of King's Inns, Dublin).
10 Ibid., p.396.

11 Minutes of 11 January 1916, Benchers' Minute Book, 1901–17, p. 419 (Library of the Honourable Society of King's Inns, Dublin).

12 Minutes of 18 January 1916, Benchers' Minute Book, 1901–17, p. 424 (Library of the Honourable Society of King's Inns, Dublin).

13 The students in question were Pangulury Sesha Thalpasaye (better known as P. S. T. Saye) and Brahmadesam Cidambi Sankara Narayana. Minutes of 9 June 1915, Benchers' Minute Book, 1901–17, p. 407 (Library of the Honourable Society of King's Inns, Dublin).

14 Minutes of 18 January 1915, Benchers' Minute Book, 1901–17, p. 391 (Library of the Honourable Society of King's Inns, Dublin).

15 Minutes of 1 November 1915, Benchers' Minute Book, 1901–17, p. 414 (Library of the Honourable Society of King's Inns, Dublin).

16 'Medical card of Aftab or Aftab-Rai' (National Archives, Kew, WO 372/1/26088).

17 British Library, 'World Wars' (Asians in Britain, online exhibition) [http://www.bl.uk/learning/histcitizen/asians/worldwars/theworldwars.html; accessed 10 November 2015].

18 See Judith M. Brown and Anthony J. Parel (eds), *The Cambridge Companion to Gandhi* (Cambridge, 2011), p. xiv.

19 Gandhi had left Britain for India in December 1914.

20 G. S. Bhargava, *V. V. Giri: Portrait of a President* (Delhi, 1970), p. 30.

21 Ibid.

22 Ibid., pp 30–1.

23 British Library, 'World Wars' (Asians in Britain, online exhibition). [http://www.bl.uk/learning/histcitizen/asians/worldwars/theworldwars.html; accessed 10 November 2015].

24 For reportage of Redmond's Woodenbridge speech, see *Freeman's Journal*, 21 September 1914.
25 Robert Michels, *Political Parties: A Sociological Study of the Oligarchical Tendencies of Modern Democracy*, ed. Seymour Lipset (1st Eng. ed., London, 1915: new ed., New Brunswick, 1999), p. 398.
26 Ibid., p. 399.

Chapter 6 – Teachers and Lectures

1 *UCD Calendar for the Session 1915–16* (Dublin, 1915), p. 322.
2 Ibid.
3 Ibid., pp 322–3.
4 Conor Mulvagh, 'The Murnaghan memos: Catholic concerns with the third Home Rule bill, 1912' in Gabriel Doherty (ed.), *The Home Rule Crisis, 1912–14* (Cork, 2014), pp 164–84.
5 Patrick Maume, 'Clery, Arthur Edward' in James McGuire and James Quinn (eds), *Dictionary of Irish Biography* (Cambridge, 2009) [accessed online 30 October 2015].
6 V. V. Giri, *My Life and Times, Volume I* (Delhi, 1976), p. 14.
7 Minutes of 8 October 1913, *University College, Dublin. Minute Book, Academic Council Book I*, November 1909 – May 1915 (IE UCDA, Gv1/1), p. 426.
8 Ibid.
9 Minutes of 29 January 1914, *University College, Dublin. Minute Book, Academic Council Book I*, November 1909 – May 1915 (IE UCDA, Gv1/1), p. 476.
10 Fergusson, *King's Inns Barristers* and *University College Dublin Calendar for the Session 1914–15* (Dublin, 1914), p. 304.
11 Minutes of 5 October 1914, *University College, Dublin. Minute Book, Academic Council Book I*, November 1909–May 1915(IE UCDA, Gv1/1), p. 516.

12 Minutes of 6 October 1914, item 7, *University College Dublin Governing Body Minute Book 3*, 20 March 1913 to 23 March 1915 (IE UCDA, GV2/3).

13 Minutes of 19 October 1914, *University College, Dublin. Minute Book, Academic Council Book I,* November 1909 – May 1915, p. 524.

14 'An Indian' [pseud.], 'The Indian Students' in *National Student: A Magazine of University Life*, iv, no. 6 (June 1914), p. 137.

15 Ibid.

16 Ibid. The Mr Dillon referred to is John Dillon, MP for Mayo East, former leader of the anti-Parnellite majority of the Irish constitutional nationalists during the 1890s and one of the most important nationalist politicians in this period. Dillon championed colonial causes in the House of Commons, especially that of Egypt, and he would go on to become the leader of the Irish Party in 1918 following the death of the party's then chairman, John Redmond, in March. See F. S. L. Lyons, *John Dillon: A Biography* (London, 1977).

17 S. R. Bakshi, *V. V. Giri: Labour Leader* (New Delhi, 1992), p. 5.

18 M. S. Purnalingam Pillai, *Ravana the Great: King of Lanka in Eleven Chapters with Map and Appendix* (Munnirpallam, The Bibliotheca, 1928).

19 M. S. Poornalingam Pillai, *Full Notes on A.T. Quiller Couch's Historical Tales from Shakespeare and Washington Irving's England's Rural Life and Christmas Customs* (Madras, P. R. Rama Ayyar & Company, 1913). For the work referred to, see Arthur Thomas Quiller-Couch, *Historical Tales from Shakespeare* (London, Edward Arnold, 1910).

20 *University College Dublin Calendar for the Session 1915–16* (Dublin, 1915), p. 146.

21 Lawrence William White, 'MacDonagh, Thomas' in James McGuire and James Quinn (eds), *Dictionary of Irish Biography* (Cambridge, 2009) [accessed online 30 October 2015].
22 Mary Shine Thompson, 'From Donovan to Donoghue: English studies at UCD' in Brian G. Caraher and Robert Mahony (eds), *Ireland and Transatlantic Poetics: Essays in Honor of Denis Donoghue* (Newark, 2007), p. 39.
23 Austin Clarke, *A Penny in the Clouds: More Memories of Ireland and England* (London, 1968), p. 25.
24 Donal McCartney, *UCD, A National Idea: The History of University College Dublin* (Dublin, 1999), p. 65.
25 Cited in Thomas J. Morrissey, 'Finlay, Thomas Aloysius' in James McGuire and James Quinn (eds), *Dictionary of Irish Biography* (Cambridge, 2009) [accessed online 30 October 2015].
26 *UCD calendar for the session 1915-16*, p. 178.
27 Ibid., pp 178–9.
28 Pauric J. Dempsey, 'Davitt, Cahir' in James McGuire and James Quinn (eds), *Dictionary of Irish Biography* (Cambridge, 2009) [accessed online 30 October 2015].
29 King's Inns Continuous Course Examination, 1915: Victoria Prizes, Junior Class, 2 June 1915 (Library of the Honourable Society of King's Inns, Dublin, L 3/5/7).
30 See Fergusson, *King's Inns Barristers*, p. 346.
31 See, for example, the papers of John A. Costello which hold very little relating to his student days across fifty-two archival boxes of material, 1914–76. (IE UCDA P190).
32 For a detailed study of tensions and prejudice in the relationship between Indian students and their classmates in English and Scottish universities, see Shompa Lahiri, *Indians in Britain: Anglo-Indian Encounters, Race, and Identity, 1880–1930* (London, 2000), pp 48–81.

33 *National Student: A Magazine of University Life*, vi, no. 1 (December 1915), p. 12.
34 G. S. Bhargava, *V. V. Giri: Portrait of a President* (Delhi, 1970), p. 39.

Chapter 7 – Student Politics: Indian Activism and Radical Irish Connections

1 V. V. Giri, *My Life and Times, Volume I* (Delhi, 1976), p. 14.
2 Ibid., p. 15.
3 Alex Tickell, 'Scholarship-terrorists: the India House Hostel and the "student problem" in Edwardian London' in Rehana Ahmed and Sumita Mukherjee (eds), *South Asian Resistances in Britain, 1858–1947* (London, 2011), p.10.
4 UCD calendar for the session 1915–16, pp 577 and 581 respectively.
5 For instance, see *Irish Volunteer,* 7 February 1914.
6 Velcheru Narayana Rao, *Hibiscus on the Lake: Twentieth-century Telugu Poetry from India* (Madison, 2003), p. 295 and V. V. B. Rama Rao, *Unnava Lakshmi Narayana* (New Delhi, 2002).
7 Record book of the Law Students' Debating Society (Library of the Honourable Society of King's Inns, Dublin).
8 Membership list for 1913–14. Record book of the Law Students' Debating Society (Library of the Honourable Society of King's Inns, Dublin), p. 52.
9 Renamed Cathal Brugha Barracks, the site remains a military barracks to this day. On the eve of the 1916 Rising, there were less than 600 soldiers quartered in the barracks although it had capacity for a greater number. *Royal Commission on the Arrest and Subsequent Treatment of Mr. Francis Sheehy Skeffington, Mr. Thomas*

Dickson, and Mr. Patrick James McIntyre. Report of commission, 3 [Cd. 8376], H.C. 1916, xi, p. 313.

10 See Giri, *Life and Times*, p. 15.

11 Ibid.

12 South Asia Microform Project (SAMP), 'Indian Proscribed Tracts, 1907–1947' [microform], Norman Gerald Barrier (compiler), Reel 16, no. 8.

13 See Giri, *Life and Times*, p. 15.

14 Ibid.

15 Akhila Jagdish, 7 January 2014, correspondence in possession of the author.

16 R. F. Foster, *Vivid Faces: The Revolutionary Generation in Ireland, 1890–1923* (London, 2014), p. 425.

17 Referenced in Maire O'Neill, *From Parnell to de Valera: A Biography of Jennie Wyse Power, 1858–1941* (Dublin, 1991), p. 75.

18 See Foster, *Vivid Faces*, p. 52.

19 For an early example of this advert, see *An Claidheamh Soluis*, 7 February 1914.

20 Dublin Metropolitan Police Detective Department, 'Information respecting the Sinn Feiners', 31 March 1916 (UKNA, CO 904/23/59).

21 Ibid.

Chapter 8 – 1916: Suspicion and Sedition

1 G. S. Bhargava, *V. V. Giri: Portrait of a President* (Delhi, 1970), p. 31. It should also be noted that Giri may not have travelled to Cork city but to rural county Cork. Berehaven in west county Cork was a significant site of naval activity both before and during the First World War. See John Ware, 'Bantry Bay in the First World War' in *History Ireland*, xiii, no. 6 (November–December 2015), pp 30–3.

2 See Bhargava, *Giri*, p. 31.

3 Richard J. Popplewell, *Intelligence and Imperial Defence: British Intelligence and the Defence of the Indian Empire, 1904–1924* (London, 1995), p. 216 *et seq.*

4 Among the India Office Records and Private Papers held at the British Library is a file on the establishment of an Indian Police deputation in England 'In consequence of the development of Indian anarchical activities in England in 1909', namely Madan Lal Dhingra's assassination of Wyllie, 2 May 1915 (British Library, IOR/L/P&J/12/36).

5 'An Indian' [pseud.], 'The Indian Students' in *National Student: A Magazine of University Life*, iv, no. 6 (June 1914), p. 137.

6 Report of John Bruton (Sergeant 5. G. [DMP]), re: 'The Eye Opener', 6 April 1916 (NAI, CSORP/1916/9070).

7 On Griffith's journalism, see Virginia E. Glandon, *Arthur Griffith and the Advanced-nationalist Press: Ireland, 1900–1922* (New York, 1985). For a digitised copy of *Scissors and Paste* online, see southdublinlibraries.ie [http://source.southdublinlibraries.ie/bitstream/10599/11418/5/19150102.pdf; accessed 12 Nov. 2015].

8 DMP Memorandum no. 11072 of 3 April 1916, (NAI, CSORP/1916/9070).

9 John Borgonovo, *The Dynamics of War and Revolution: Cork City, 1916–1918* (Cork, 2013), pp 122–26.

10 Ibid., p. 125.

11 Ibid.

12 Ibid., p. 126.

13 Frank McNally, 'Meanwhile, in other news' [Irishman's Diary], *Irish Times*, 19 April 2013. The Royal Commission of Inquiry into the circumstances of Skeffington's arrest and murder saw fit to point out Dickson's physical appearance also, describing him as 'a Scotchman, and deformed'. *Royal Commission on the Arrest and Subsequent Treatment of Mr. Francis Sheehy*

Skeffington, Mr. Thomas Dickson, and Mr. Patrick James McIntyre. Report of commission, 6 [Cd. 8376], H.C. 1916, xi, p. 316.

14 Statement of Michael Noyk (Military Archives of Ireland, BMH, WS 707), p. 8.

15 *Eye-Opener*, 18 and 25 March 1916.

16 Hastings D. Draper, solicitor, to Matthew Nathan, 29 March 1916 (NAI, CSORP/1916/5561).

17 *Eye-Opener*, 18 March 1916.

18 *Eye-Opener*, 25 March 1916.

19 Ibid.

20 Ibid.

21 Evidence of Ensign Dennis Ryan, US Navy, 9 Sept. 1917, cited in Borgonovo, *The Dynamics of War and Revolution*, p. 129.

22 *Eye-Opener*, 25 March 1916.

23 Ibid. 'Céad míle fáilte' is an Irish phrase meaning 'a hundred thousand welcomes' which has become an embedded part of the Irish notion of hospitality.

24 Ibid.

25 *Eye-Opener*, 1 April 1916. Phibsboro'/Phibsborough is one of the inner northern suburbs of Dublin city.

26 DMP Memorandum no. 11072 of 3 April 1916, (NAI, CSORP/1916/9070). On the longer history of racial abuse being directed at Indians on the streets of Britain, see Rozina Visram, *Ayahs, Lascars, and Princes: Indians in Britain: 1700–1947* (London, 1986), pp 182–3.

27 D. R. Kalia to Private Secretary to the Lord Lieutenant of Ireland, n.d. [received 28 March 1916], (NAI, CSORP/1916/9070).

28 B. N. Mahant to Private Secretary to the Lord Lieutenant of Ireland, 28 March 1916 (NAI, CSORP/1916/9070).

29 DMP Memorandum no. 3262 of 6 April 1916, (NAI, CSORP/1916/9070).

30 *Irish Independent*, 13 April 1916.

31 *Eye-Opener*, 15 April 1916.
32 'Here we are again!', *Eye-Opener*, 15 April 1916.
33 Abdur Razzaq to Private Secretary to the Lord Lieutenant of Ireland [Viscount Wimborne], 19 April 1916 (NAI, CSORP/1916/9070).
34 See Giri, *Life and Times*, p. 26.
35 P. S. T. Sayee [Pangulury Sesha Thalpasaye] to Éamon de Valera, 12 June 1948 (Frank Aiken Papers, IE UCDA, P104/4806), quoted in Kate O'Malley, *Ireland, India and Empire: Indo-Irish Radical Connections, 1919–64* (Manchester, 2008), p. 167.
36 On Garret FitzGerald's correspondence with O'Malley, see O'Malley, *Ireland, India and Empire*, p. 177[n].
37 *Eye-Opener*, 22 April 1916.
38 *Eye-Opener*, 22 April 1916.
39 Ibid.
40 Register of members, 1915–16, Record book of the Law Students' Debating Society (Library of the Honourable Society of King's Inns, Dublin).
41 *Eye-Opener*, 22 April 1916.
42 See *Royal Commission on the Arrest and Subsequent Treatment of Mr. Francis Sheehy Skeffington, Mr. Thomas Dickson, and Mr. Patrick James McIntyre. Report of commission*, 6 [Cd. 8376], H.C. 1916, xi, p. 316 and Patrick Maume, 'Colthurst, John Colthurst Bowen-' in James McGuire and James Quinn (eds), *Dictionary of Irish Biography* (Cambridge, 2009) [accessed online 30 October 2015].
43 *Royal Commission on the Arrest and Subsequent Treatment of Mr. Francis Sheehy Skeffington, Mr. Thomas Dickson, and Mr. Patrick James McIntyre. Report of commission*, 3-6 [Cd. 8376], H.C. 1916, xi, 313–16. J. J. Kelly should not be confused with his fellow Dublin City Councillor, Alderman Tom Kelly, a member of Sinn Féin who famously read the so-called 'Castle Document'

to a meeting of the City Council on 20 April 1916. See 'Irishman's Diary', *Irish Times*, 23 February 2004 and Sheila Carden, *The Alderman: Alderman Tom Kelly (1868–1942) and Dublin Corporation* (Dublin, 2007). See also Brian Mahon, 'Kelly's Corner and 1916' [letter to the editor], *Irish Times*, 27 June 2015.

44 *Royal Commission on the Arrest and Subsequent Treatment of Mr. Francis Sheehy Skeffington, Mr. Thomas Dickson, and Mr. Patrick James McIntyre. Report of commission*, 5 [Cd. 8376], H.C. 1916, xi, p. 315.

45 *Irish Times*, 28 August 1916; *Irish Examiner*, 28 August 1916.

46 Virginia E. Glandon, *Arthur Griffith and the Advanced-nationalist Press: Ireland, 1900–1922* (New York, 1985), p. 111.

47 Padraig Yeates, *A City in Wartime: Dublin 1914–1918* (Dublin, 2011), p. 113.

48 The last issue of *The Toiler* held at the National Library of Ireland is vol. 2, no. 12 (19 December 1914).

49 *Meath Chronicle*, 26 September 1914.

50 *Meath Chronicle*, 22 April 1916.

51 See the back pages of the *Eye-Opener*, following the hiatus in the paper's publication, there were no adverts in the four page special edition published on 15 April. On 22 April, the last issue, Kelly's advert reappears on the final (eighth) page, *Eye-Opener*, 22 April 1916.

52 D. R. Kalia to Private Secretary to the Lord Lieutenant of Ireland, n.d. [received 28 March 1916], (NAI, CSORP/1916/9070).

53 Antoinette Burton, *At the Heart of the Empire: Indians and the Colonial Encounter in Late-Victorian Britain* (Berkeley, 1998), p. 189, emphasis as per Burton's original text.

54 *Irish Times*, 15 May 1916.

55 See Giri, *Life and Times*, pp 32–3.

56 On the Bengal Nagpur Railway strike, see Bhargava, *Giri*, pp 40–56.
57 See Bhargava, *Giri*, pp 49–51.

Chapter 9 – Leaving Ireland

1 V. V. Giri, *My Life and Times, Volume I* (Delhi, 1976), p. 33.
2 Ibid.
3 Ibid.
4 *Hansard 5 (Commons)*, lxxxii, cols 2922–3 (1 June 1916).
5 Ben Johnson, 'Empire Day', *Historic UK* [http://www.historic-uk.com/HistoryUK/HistoryofBritain/Empire-Day; accessed 11 November 2015].
6 See Giri, *Life and Times*, p. 33.
7 Minutes of 21 June 1916, Benchers' Minute Book, 1901–17, p. 440 (Library of the Honourable Society of King's Inns, Dublin).
8 See Giri, *Life and Times*, p. 33.
9 Ibid., pp 33–4.
10 *Irish Times*, 14 June 1917.
11 *Irish Times*, 30 June 1917.
12 *Ibid.*
13 G. S. Bhargava, *V. V. Giri: Portrait of a President* (Delhi, 1970), pp 35–6.
14 See Bhargava, *Giri*, p. 39. See also Narasingha P. Sil, 'Giri, Varahagiri Venkata (1894–1980)', *Oxford Dictionary of National Biography* (Oxford, 2008) [http://www.oxforddnb.com/view/article/93404; accessed 7 January 2014].
15 *Irish Times*, 29 Nov. 1916.
16 Ibid.
17 *The Tribune* [India, Eng. Edn.], 13 April 2002.
18 Indian National Congress, *Report of the Commissioners appointed by the Punjab Sub-Committee of the Indian National Congress* (Bombay, 1920), p. 50.

19 B. Seshagiri Rao, *History of the Freedom Movement in Guntur District, 1921–47* (Ongole, n.d.), p. 105.
20 Rao, *History of the Freedom Movement*, p. 56.
21 Ibid., p.129.
22 See Sil, 'Giri' and Bhargava, *Giri*.

Conclusion

1 Éamon de Valera, *India and Ireland* (New York, 1920), p. 3.
2 Maia Ramnath, *Haj to Utopia: How the Ghadar Movement Charted Global Radicalism and Attempted to Overthrow the British Empire* (Berkeley, 2011). A photograph of the sword and flag appears in Kate O'Malley, *Ireland, India, and Empire: Indo-Irish Radical Connections, 1919–64* (Manchester, 2008), p. 125.
3 Press clippings of the presentation are included in Cuairt Oifigiuil, Uachtarán nah Indie (NAI, PRES 2005/3/144).
4 Embassy of Ireland, Delhi, Confidential Report P. R. 6/72, 'President Giri & Ireland', 28 January 1972 (NAI DFA 2001/27/365).
5 Embassy of Ireland, Delhi, Confidential Report P. R. 6/72, 'President Giri & Ireland', 28 January 1972 (NAI DFA 2001/27/365).
6 On Iremonger, see Bridget Hourican, 'Iremonger, Valentin' in James McGuire and James Quinn (eds), *Dictionary of Irish Biography* (Cambridge, 2009) [accessed online 30 October 2015].
7 Embassy of Ireland, Delhi, Confidential Report P. R. 6/72, 'President Giri & Ireland', 28 January 1972 (NAI DFA 2001/27/365).
8 'Proposed Visit of President of India', 21 January 1974 (NAI, PRES 2005/3/144).
9 Embassy of Ireland, Delhi, Confidential Report P. R. 23/74, 'Indian Presidential Election', 5 July 1974 (NAI

DFA 2009/89/21).

10 Giri's desire to meet de Valera is explicitly reported in an official note of 21 January 1974: 'Proposed Visit of President of India', 21 January 1974 (NAI, PRES 2005/3/144).

Bibliography

Primary sources

Archival sources

British Library

India Office Records and Private Papers, India Office: Public and Judicial Department Records 1795–1950 (IOR/L/P&J/12)

Honourable Society of King's Inns, Library

Benchers' Minute Book, 1901–17

King's Inns Continuous Course Examination, 1915: Victoria Prizes, examination results (L 3/5/7)

Record book of the Law Students' Debating Society

Military Archives of Ireland

Bureau of Military History

Molony, Helena, WS 391

Noyk, Michael, WS 707

O'Hegarty, Patrick Sarsfield, WS 839

Ua Caomhánaigh, Seamus, WS 889

National Archives of Ireland

Chief Secretary's Office Registered Papers

Department of Foreign Affairs series

President of Ireland (Uachtarán na hÉireann) series

Trinity College Dublin, Department of Manuscripts

Entrance books, 1896–1915 (TCD MUN/V/24)

United Kingdom National Archives, Kew

Chief Secretary's Office papers, Dublin Metropolitan Police Detective Department series (CO 904/23)

War Office: Service Medal and Award Rolls Index, First World War (WO 372)

University College Dublin Archives

Frank Aiken papers, P 104

John A. Costello papers, P 190

University College, Dublin. Minute Book, Academic Council Book I, November 1909 – May 1915 (IE UCDA, Gv1/1)

UCD Governing Body Minute Book 3, 20 March 1913 to 23 March 1915 (IE, UCDA, GV2/3)

UCD Governing Body Minute Book 4, 23 March 1915 to 20 March 1917 (IE, UCDA, GV2/4)

Newspapers

An Claidheamh Soluis

Bean na hÉireann

Eye-Opener

Freeman's Journal

Hindu, (The)

Irish Examiner

Irish Independent

Irish Times

Irish Volunteer

Meath Chronicle

National Student: A Magazine of University Life

Scissors and Paste

Toiler, (The)

Tribune, (The) [India, English Edition]

Official publications

Dublin University Calendar for the year 1912–13, Vol. II (Dublin, 1913).

The parliamentary debates (Hansard), fifth series, House of Commons (London).

East India (Indian Students' Department). Report on the Work of the Indian Students' Department, July 1913–June 1914, 1–17 [Cd 7719], H.C. 1914–16, xlviii, pp 3–19.

Royal Commission on the Arrest and Subsequent Treatment of Mr. Francis Sheehy Skeffington, Mr. Thomas Dickson, and Mr. Patrick James McIntyre. Report of commission, 1–12 [Cd. 8376], H.C. 1916, xi, pp 311–22.

University College Dublin Calendar for the Session 1914–15 (Dublin, 1914).

University College Dublin Calendar for the Session 1915–16 (Dublin, 1915).

University College Dublin Calendar for the Session 1916–17 (Dublin, 1916).

University College Dublin Calendar for the Session 1917–18 (Dublin, 1917).

Contemporary printed sources

Chettiar, T. Adinarayana, 'Esperants [sic] – What can it do for India', *East and West*, iv, no. 47 (September 1905).

De Valera, Éamon, *India and Ireland* (New York, 1920).

Indian National Congress, *Report of the Commissioners appointed by the Punjab Sub-Committee of the Indian National Congress* (Bombay, 1920).

Luzac's Oriental List Volume XVI, January to December 1905 (Chicago, 1905).

Michels, Robert, *Political Parties: A Sociological Study of the Oligarchical Tendencies of Modern Democracy*, ed. Seymour Lipset (1st Eng. ed., London, 1915: new ed., New Brunswick, 1999).

Pillai, M. S. Purnalingam, *Full Notes on A.T. Quiller Couch's Historical Tales from Shakespeare and Washington Irving's England's Rural Life and Christmas Customs* (Madras, P. R. Rama Ayyar & Company, 1913).

Pillai, M. S. Purnalingam, *Ravana the Great: King of Lanka in Eleven Chapters with Map and Appendix* (Munnirpallam: The Bibliotheca, 1928).

Quiller-Couch, Arthur Thomas, *Historical Tales from Shakespeare* (London: Edward Arnold, 1910).

Tagore, Rabindranath, *Gitanjali (Song Offerings): a Collection of Prose Translations made by the Author from the Original Bengali* (London, 1912).

Secondary sources

Bakshi, S. R., *V. V. Giri: Labour Leader* (New Delhi, 1992).

Bhargava, G. S., *V. V. Giri: Portrait of a President* (Delhi, 1970).

Borgonovo, John, *The Dynamics of War and Revolution: Cork City, 1916–1918* (Cork, 2013).

Brown, Judith M., and Anthony J. Parel (eds), *The Cambridge Companion to Gandhi* (Cambridge, 2011).

Bu, Liping, 'The Challenge of Race Relations: American Ecumenism and Foreign Student Nationalism, 1900–1940', *Journal of American Studies*, xxxv, no. 2 (August, 2001), pp 217–237.

Burton, Antoinette, *At the Heart of the Empire: Indians and the Colonial Encounter in Late-Victorian Britain* (Berkeley, 1998).

Carden, Sheila, *The Alderman: Alderman Tom Kelly (1868–1942) and Dublin Corporation* (Dublin, 2007).

Clarke, Austin, *A Penny in the Clouds: More Memories of Ireland and England* (London, 1968).

Fergusson, Kenneth (ed.), *King's Inns Barristers, 1868–2004* (Dublin, 2005).

Foster, R. F., *Vivid Faces: The Revolutionary Generation in Ireland, 1890–1923* (London, 2014).

Giri, V. V., *My Life and Times, Volume I* (Delhi, 1976).

Glandon, Virginia E., *Arthur Griffith and the Advanced-nationalist Press: Ireland, 1900–1922* (New York, 1985).

Hanna, Martha, 'French Women and American Men: "Foreign" Students at the University of Paris, 1915–1925', *French Historical Studies*, xxii, no. 1 (Winter, 1999), pp 87–112.

Hessler, Julie, 'Death of an African Student in Moscow: Race, Politics, and the Cold War', *Cahiers du Monde Russe*, xlvii, no. 1/2, (January - June, 2006), pp 33–63.

Kennedy, Michael, '"Where's the Taj Mahal?": Indian restaurants in Dublin since 1908', *History Ireland*, xviii, no. 4, [special issue: 'The Elephant and Partition: Ireland and India'] (July/August 2010), pp 50–2.

Khan, Adil Hussain, 'Muslim students in 1950s Dublin', *History Ireland*, xviii, no. 4, [special issue: 'The Elephant and Partition: Ireland and India'] (July/August 2010), pp 44–5.

Laffan, Michael, 'The emergence of the "Two Irelands", 1912–25', *History Ireland*, xii, no. 4 (Winter 2004), pp 40–44.

Lahiri, Shompa, *Indians in Britain: Anglo-Indian Encounters, Race, and Identity, 1880–1930* (London, 2000).

Lyons, F. S. L., *John Dillon: A Biography* (London, 1977).

McCartney, Donal, *UCD, A National Idea: The History of University College Dublin* (Dublin, 1999).

Mulvagh, Conor, 'The Murnaghan memos: Catholic concerns with the third Home Rule bill, 1912' in Gabriel Doherty (ed.), *The Home Rule Crisis, 1912–14* (Cork, 2014), pp 164–84.

Nordbruch, Goetz, 'Arab Students in Weimar Germany – Politics and Thought Beyond Borders', *Journal of Contemporary History*, xlix, no. 2 (April 2014), pp 275–295.

O'Malley, Kate, *Ireland, India and Empire: Indo-Irish Radical Connections, 1919–64* (Manchester, 2008).

O'Neill, Maire, *From Parnell to de Valera: A Biography of Jennie Wyse Power, 1858–1941* (Dublin, 1991).

Popplewell, Richard J., *Intelligence and Imperial Defence: British Intelligence and the Defence of the Indian Empire, 1904–1924* (London, 1995).

Posadas, Barbara M. and Roland L. Guyotte, 'Unintentional Immigrants: Chicago's Filipino Foreign Students Become Settlers, 1900–1941', *Journal of American Ethnic History*, ix, no. 2 (Spring, 1990).

Ramnath, Maia, *Haj to Utopia: How the Ghadar Movement Charted Global Radicalism and Attempted to Overthrow the British Empire* (Berkeley, 2011).

Rao, B. Seshagiri, *History of the Freedom Movement in Guntur District, 1921–47* (Ongole, n.d.).

Rao, V. V. B. Rama, *Unnava Lakshmi Narayana* (New Delhi, 2002).

Rao, Velcheru Narayana, *Hibiscus on the Lake: Twentieth-century Telugu Poetry from India* (Madison, 2003).

Sen, Malcolm, 'Mythologising a "Mystic": W. B. Yeats on the poetry of Rabindranath Tagore', *History Ireland*, xviii, no. 4, [special issue: 'The Elephant and Partition: Ireland and India'] (July/August 2010), pp 20–3.

Thompson, Mary Shine, 'From Donovan to Donoghue: English studies at UCD' in Brian G. Caraher and Robert Mahony (eds), *Ireland and Transatlantic Poetics: Essays in Honor of Denis Donoghue* (Newark, 2007).

Tickell, Alex, 'Scholarship-terrorists: the India House Hostel and the "student problem" in Edwardian London' in Rehana Ahmed and Sumita Mukherjee (eds), *South Asian Resistances in Britain, 1858–1947* (London, 2011), pp 3–18.

Visram, Rozina, *Ayahs, Lascars, and Princes: Indians in Britain: 1700–1947* (London, 1986).

Walker, Brian M., *Parliamentary Election Results in Ireland, 1801–1922* (Dublin, 1978).

Ware, John, 'Bantry Bay in the First World War' in *History Ireland*, xiii, no. 6 (November–December 2015), pp 30–3.

Weber, Thomas, *Our Friend 'The Enemy': Elite Education in Britain and Germany before World War I* (Stanford, 2008).

Yeates, Padraig, *A City in Wartime: Dublin 1914–1918* (Dublin, 2011).

Dictionary of Irish Biography, James McGuire and James Quinn (eds) (9 vols, Cambridge, 2009; online ed., 2009, dib.cambridge.org)

Dempsey, Pauric J., 'Davitt, Cahir'
Hourican, Bridget, 'Iremonger, Valentin'
Maume, Patrick 'Clery, Arthur Edward'
Maume, Patrick, 'Colthurst, John Colthurst Bowen-'
Morrissey, Thomas J., 'Finlay, Thomas Aloysius'
White, Lawrence William, 'MacDonagh, Thomas'

Oxford Dictionary of National Biography, H.C.G. Matthew and Brian Harrison (eds) (Oxford, 2004; online ed., Jan. 2008, oxforddnb.com)

Brown, F. H., 'Warner, Sir William Lee- (1846–1914)', rev. Katherine Prior
Ives, E. W., 'Henry VIII (1491–1547)'
Sil, Narasingha P., 'Giri, Varahagiri Venkata (1894–1980)'

Other online resources

1911 census [see www.census.nationalarchives.ie].

British Library, 'World Wars' (Asians in Britain, online exhibition) [http://www.bl.uk/learning/histcitizen/asians/worldwars/theworldwars.html].

Central Statistics Office, *Census 2011 Profile 6: Migration and Diversity – A Profile of Diversity in Ireland* (Dublin, 2012) [http://www.cso.ie/en/media/csoie/census/documents/census2011profile6/Profile,6,Migration,and,Diversity,entire,doc.pdf].

Clydebuilt Ships Database [clydesite.co.uk/clydebuilt].

Interview with Sydney Gifford Czira (19 May 1971), RTÉ Archives [http://www.rte.ie/archives/2014/0402/606021-cumann-na-mban-and-anti-women-irb/].

Irish Government News Service [press release], 'Minister Flanagan welcomes gift of WB Yeats bust to be presented to India', 10 September 2014 [http://www.merrionstreet.ie/en/News-Room/Releases/minister-flanagan-welcomes-gift-of-wb-yeats-bust-to-be-presented-to-india.html].

Johnson, Ben, 'Empire Day', *Historic UK* [http://www.historic-uk.com/HistoryUK/HistoryofBritain/Empire-Day].

South Asia Microform Project (SAMP), 'Indian Proscribed Tracts, 1907–1947' [microform] [https://www.crl.edu/programs/samp].

South Dublin Libraries [southdublinlibraries.ie].

Index